$6 18.—

D1544206

Revenue Sharing

Revenue Sharing

Methodological Approaches and Problems

Edited by

David A. Caputo
Purdue University

Richard L. Cole
The George Washington University

Lexington Books
D.C. Heath and Company
Lexington, Massachusetts
Toronto

Library of Congress Cataloging in Publication Data

Main entry under title:
Revenue sharing.

Includes indexes.
 1. Revenue sharing—United States—Addresses, essays, lectures.
I. Caputo, David A., 1943-   II. Cole, Richard L.
HF 275.R387   336.1'85   75-45862
ISBN 0-669-00238-0

Published simultaneously in Canada

Printed in the United States of America

International Standard Book Number: 0-669-00238-0

Library of Congress Catalog Card Number: 75-45862

For our Families

Contents

viii

Profaoo

In October of 1972, after more than a decade of public and academic debate, Congress passed and President Nixon signed the general revenue sharing bill. Dispensing over $30 billion to states and localities over the five-year life of the program, the measure was to have important fiscal consequences for state and local governments, many of which were facing severe economic hardships. As significant as were its fiscal consequences, the political impacts of general revenue sharing were even more profound. Unlike the categorical grant programs of previous years, which tended to centralize decision making in Washington, general revenue sharing represented the allocation of almost unrestricted funds—money local officials could use as they saw fit, unencumbered by nationally imposed guidelines. For some, this flexibility was viewed as providing local decision makers with the opportunity to apply the money in areas of critical local needs. For others, this meant the possible abandonment of many hard-fought national goals such as the elimination of poverty, the provision of quality housing and economic opportunities, and the opportunity for politically and socially disadvantaged citizens to participate in a variety of nationally defined programs.

Given the importance of the revenue sharing measure, it is not surprising that public, academic, and professional interest in the program exceeded that of almost any previous domestic policy. Many of the important revenue sharing research efforts are discussed in this book and need not be reviewed at this point; however, to those interested in revenue sharing research, the question of how to carry out appropriately inquiry in this area became almost as important as the substantive issues of the act. Should revenue sharing be studied from an economic, political, or social perspective? Should interviews be conducted with state and local officials or with groups of local citizens? Should the research be conducted on an aggregate or case study basis? Should research techniques be of the questionnaire variety, or should in-depth interviews be conducted? Should researchers focus on the planned and actual use reports filed by public officials, or should these be ignored in favor of more sophisticated economic projection studies? These and many other methodological questions have been of intense interest and controversy to revenue sharing researchers.

Regardless of the technique selected, for all groups involved in the study of revenue sharing the research has involved major allocations of time and financial resources. Much of this research now is complete, and much has reached the attention of both the general public and decision makers considering the renewal of the legislation. At the same time, a considerable amount of thoughtful research, using a variety of approaches, has not received critical evaluation and consideration.

This book brings together a variety of six original essays (chapters 1–6) by persons active in ongoing general revenue sharing research and also offers three overview essays (chapters 7–9) on the nature and quality of the research to date. The editors solicited these manuscripts in an attempt to provide as diverse and as representative an array of approaches, positions, and conclusions as possible regarding general revenue sharing.

In addition, the study of general revenue sharing raises a series of important methodological and substantive questions concerning the impact and utility of policy analysis and research in the context of ongoing governmental programs. We raise those questions and attempt to pose answers in our concluding chapter. We urge the reader to view the collection not only as providing substantive answers to the impact of general revenue sharing, but also as a series of specific criticisms and alternative approaches as to how to measure the impact and policy implications of the program. We feel these chapters, coupled with the variety of more substantive material available, provide a thorough and useful overview of the various methodological approaches used to investigate general revenue sharing.

We would like to thank the contributors, each of whom faithfully kept our deadlines and prepared well-done contributions. In addition, we would like to acknowledge the support we received from Purdue University and The George Washington University, which enabled us to compile and edit this work. The personnel at Lexington Books, especially Mike McCarroll, made our task enjoyable by providing us the support and encouragement needed. As the dedication indicates, we would like to thank our families who understood our preoccupation with mail deliveries and chapter word counts. Finally, we would like to thank the public officials and private citizens who participated in and were affected by the various research attempts summarized here. Our hope is that they are the ultimate benefactors of this effort.

Introduotion

David A. Caputo and Richard L. Cole

In 1971 President Richard M. Nixon called for legislative approval of a
broad range of new programs labeled the "New Federalism" and
contended that the enactment of these programs would result in "A New
American Revolution—a peaceful revolution in which power is turned
back to the people . . . a revolution as profound, as far reaching, as exciting
as the first revolution almost 200 years ago."[1] Nixon went on to argue that
in just ". . . five years America [can] enter its third century as a young
nation, new in spirit, with all the vigor and the freshness with which it
began its first century."[2] While few social scientists and public officials
would conclude that the New Federalism, as typified by general revenue
sharing, has resulted in such dramatic changes in the past five years, it is
apparent to most that the concepts and specific programs of the
Nixon–Ford administrations have resulted in a shift in the nature of
intergovernmental relationships in this country and that this shift may
have significant long-run implications for public policy choices in the
United States.

One of the most overlooked facts about general revenue sharing is
that the debate concerning it and the legislation itself can be justified
from a variety of different perspectives and underlying value systems. To
speak of simplistic pro and con arguments concerning general revenue
sharing is to ignore the complexities that characterize this program. This
introduction describes the general revenue sharing legislation and raises
the theoretical and methodological points needed to place the following
contributions into proper perspective.

For a program that has resulted in such intense and widespread public
debate, the State and Local Fiscal Assistance Act of 1972 is a
straightforward and unambiguous legislative act. The legislation calls for
the distribution of $30.2 billion to the more than 37,000 states, counties,
cities, towns, townships, Indian tribes, and Alaskan native villages.[a] The
general revenue sharing funds have been appropriated from federal
income tax receipts and held in a trust fund by the Treasury Department
with payments from that fund defined by statutory formula and not
subject to yearly congressional appropriations. One-third of the total
general revenue sharing funds go to the states and two-thirds to the units
of local government using formulas based on population, tax effort, and
personal income (two different formulas are used and recipient units

---

[a] For background information dealing with the goals and objectives of general revenue
sharing, see Graham W. Watt, "The Goals and Objectives of General Revenue Sharing,"
The Annals, vol. 419 (May 1975), pp. 12–22.

receive the higher of the two allocations). The funds are distributed quarterly and the recipient units must:

1. File planned and actual use reports of how the funds are going to be and were used
2. Use separate fiscal accounting procedures for the general revenue sharing funds
3. Not use the funds for programs that discriminate against persons on the ground of race, color, sex, or national origin
4. Expend general revenue sharing funds in accordance with the laws and procedures applicable to the expenditures of the government's own revenues
5. Not violate existing federal wage and labor laws
6. Use the funds (state only) for any public purpose as defined by state law
7. Use (local governments) their general revenue sharing funds for items in the following eight priority expenditures categories:
   a. Public safety
   b. Environmental protection
   c. Public transportation
   d. Health
   e. Recreation
   f. Libraries
   g. Social services for the poor or aged
   h. Financial administration

The above discussion should make it clear that general revenue sharing was indeed an attempt to ". . . place responsibility for local functions under local control and to provide local governments with the authority and resources they need to serve their communities effectively. . . ."[3] In addition, general revenue sharing was seen as an alternative approach to the problems of federal aid to states and localities when contrasted with prior categorical aid programs that stressed local and state governments complying with federal regulations prior to receipt of the federal funds.

A careful analysis of the legislative history of the revenue sharing program indicates it meant different things to different people and in fact may have enjoyed much of its popularity because of this unique characteristic.[4] Will Meyers, writing on this topic, points out four commonly made justifications for the legislation. These include:

1. An alternative to the categorical federal grant
2. A method to provide an impetus to the economy at a nonfederal level

3. A way of decreasing the administrative costs of the categorical-aid programs
4. Providing the desperately needed funds for local government survival[5]

In addition, general revenue sharing has been conceived as a way to:

1. Increase citizen participation
2. Increase the power and authority of local governmental officials
3. Permit funding to solve problems rather than funding that defines problems
4. Shift the power and authority that had been flowing to the federal government back to the states and localities.[b]

A comparable list of arguments against general revenue sharing could be offered, but the main point should be stressed. General revenue sharing has meant different things to different people and often one's final position on its ultimate merit depends upon the various trade-offs made by the observer among what may be conflicting values. For instance, the conservative may want congressional oversight of revenue sharing expenditures since they involve federal funds, but also may value greater responsibility at the local level. The liberal may favor increased federal spending to assist large American cities, but may dislike the fact that the decision on the social programs will be made by local officials without mandatory citizen participation. Thus, proponents and opponents of general revenue sharing are likely to cite the features of the program most supportive of their own views and ignore those with which they disagree.

This raises an important and interesting question for the researchers attempting to measure the impacts of general revenue sharing. Should they evaluate the program in terms of its totality or is it reasonable to offer recommendations based only on the particular jurisdiction or category of jurisdiction under investigation? Put another way, can the researcher make a general conclusion unless each part of the program has been carefully investigated? This is the situation: Various researchers have investigated the impact of general revenue sharing, but usually from a perspective that limits the applicability of their findings or that involves their own set of values and expectations about the program. In this fashion, their recommendations to public decision makers seeking "impartial" evidence of program success or failure may be affected by their own values and views. Thus, just as was the case during the initial

---

[b] For discussion of these points, see Michael D. Reagan, "The Pro and Con Arguments," *The Annals*, vol. 419 (May 1975), pp. 23–35.

debate on the legislation, the research efforts often reflect certain underlying values and assumptions and have resulted in empirical evidence to support a wide variety of positions and stands.

This book cannot raise all of these questions nor explore all of their possible answers and ramification, but it does raise and explore the most important. The reader needs to be aware of this contextual setting and its influence on the research that follows. As editors, we have attempted to bring together a diverse set of research attempts that characterize other research efforts in these areas:

1. County and small community responses to general revenue sharing
2. Aggregate expenditure patterns as measured by the required actual use reports
3. Differing methodological approaches to the study of urban decision making in a regional area
4. SMSA distributional and decision-making patterns
5. Citizen impact on general revenue sharing decision making
6. Alternative allocation possibilities under formula research
7. An analysis of various approaches to the study of intergovernmental aid transfers
8. An evaluation of the policy applicability of the general revenue sharing research
9. An analysis and consideration of the broader questions general revenue sharing and the research dealing with it have raised

The chapters cover a wide range of approaches and conclusions often offered by revenue sharing researchers. In addition to the range of research summarized in the first six chapters, three other research projects need to be briefly summarized here since each has investigated the impact of general revenue sharing since 1972.

The first is the Caputo–Cole study involving expenditure decisions and public official attitudes towards the impact of general revenue sharing. The results of the first two years of our yearly questionnaire surveys can be found in *Urban Politics and Decentralization: The Case of General Revenue Sharing;*[6] results of subsequent surveys and a related study dealing with community action programs and general revenue sharing are also available.[7] Our main interest was in ascertaining the specific allocation of general revenue sharing funds, their perceived impact on citizen participation, tax rates, local social welfare programs, and the overall evaluation of local officials of general revenue sharing.

A second major research effort, not specifically summarized in the ensuing chapters, is the Brookings monitoring effort headed by Richard Nathan. The Brookings study included 65 jurisdictions ranging from a single Indian tribe to 29 separate municipalities in 18 different states.[8] Twenty-seven Brookings associates, drawn from a diverse set of backgrounds, but stressing the social sciences, were involved in the field work in each of the jurisdictions. Brookings received considerable foundation and governmental support for its research, and its first volume, *Monitoring Revenue Sharing,* explores the distributional, fiscal, and political effects of the program through mid-1974. Brookings has indicated its intention of producing a yearly volume, but the second one is not yet available.

Finally, the National Clearinghouse on Revenue Sharing was established in late 1973 by the National Urban Coalition, the Center for Community Change, the Center for National Policy Review, and the League of Women Voters with the expressed intent of gathering and disseminating information of general revenue sharing as well as focusing attention on the civil rights and citizen participation issues involved in the program. The clearinghouse has undertaken a variety or research projects that have attempted to be more advocacy oriented than most other research in this area. The reader interested in important research dealing with general revenue sharing would do well to review the congressional testimony and the publications of the National Clearinghouse.

With these introductory comments in mind, it is appropriate to consider the various approaches and positions developed and described in the ensuing chapters.

Notes

1. Richard M. Nixon, Annual Message to the Congress on the State of the Union, January 22, 1971.

2. Ibid.

3. October 20, 1972 remarks by Richard M. Nixon at signing of P. L. 92-512 (The State and Local Fiscal Assistance Act of 1972); see Weekly Compilation of Presidential Documents.

4. See David A. Caputo and Richard L. Cole, *Urban Politics and Decentralization: The Case of General Revenue Sharing* (Lexington, Mass: Lexington Books, D.C. Heath and Co., 1974), pp. 17–65; Richard P. Nathan, Allen D. Manvel, and Susannah E. Calkins, *Monitoring Revenue Sharing* (Washington: Brookings Institution, 1975), pp. 13–33, pp. 344–91; and Will S. Meyers, "A Legislative History of Revenue Sharing," *The Annals,* vol. 419 (May 1975), pp. 2–11.

5. Meyers, "A Legislative History of Revenue Sharing," p. 2.

6. See Caputo and Cole, *Urban Politics and Decentralization.*

7. See David A. Caputo and Richard L. Cole, Testimony to General Revenue Sharing Subcommittee of the Senate Finance Committee, April 17, 1975; and David A. Caputo and Richard L. Cole, Testimony to the Intergovernmental Relations and Human Resources Subcommittee of the House of Representative on Governmental Operations, November 12, 1975; David A. Caputo and Richard L. Cole, "General Revenue Sharing: An Epitaph for Federally Funded Anti-Poverty Programs?", paper presented at the 1976 Midwest Political Science Association meetings.

8. See Nathan, Manvel, and Calkins, *Monitoring Revenue Sharing.*

Part I
Present Research Attempts

1

Small Community Policy Making and the Revenue Sharing Program

Alvin D. Sokolow

The shifts of responsibility and power implied in the revenue sharing and other New Federalism programs have a special significance for the many local governments in small communities. Generally ignored in the implementation of the federal aid programs of the past two decades, the thousands of smaller counties, cities, and townships are now major beneficiaries of the 1972 general revenue sharing program. All general-purpose local governments—big cities and counties as well—gained new money through revenue sharing. But in relation to prior direct distributions of federal aid, units in nonmetropolitan areas gained the most.

Revenue sharing has produced a redistribution of federal aid from large to small governments, as table 1-1 suggests. Nonmetropolitan governments received about 30 percent of the first calendar year's total revenue sharing allocations to local governments, a doubling of their previous share of direct federal payments. The comparable percentages of the governments in metropolitan areas dropped from 85 percent of total direct federal aid in 1971-72 to 70 percent of revenue sharing allocations in calendar 1972. Moreover, the revenue sharing funds paid to the nonmetropolitan governments in the first year *exceeded* their total direct annual revenues from all other federal sources—by about $400 million or 38 percent.

The peculiar characteristics of the allocation formula written into the 1972 State and Local Fiscal Assistance Act certainly help out the smaller governments of the nation.[a] But these jurisdictions also gain in a more

---

[a] Many smaller local governments benefit particularly from the provision in the 1972 act that provides a minimum entitlement, equal to 20 percent of the average per capita revenue sharing grant in the state, to units that would otherwise not qualify because of the operation of the income and taxation parts of the formula. At the same time, some small governments are ineligible to receive funds because of other formula provisions—including the prohibition on a unit receiving funds equal to more than one half of its total nonschool tax and intergovernmental revenues. For a thorough discussion of formula issues, see Richard P. Nathan, Allen D. Manvel, and Susannah E. Calkins, *Monitoring Revenue Sharing* (Washington: The Brookings Institution, 1975), chapters 6 and 10.

4

Table 1–1

Redistributive Consequences of General Revenue Sharing: Direct Federal Payments to Local Governments Inside and Outside Metropolitan Areas

| | Total Direct Federal Payments to All Local Governments[a] | | | | R. S. Allocations For 1972 | | |
| | 1966–67 | | 1971–72[b] | | | | |
	Amount (mill)	Percent	Amount (mill)	Percent	Number of Local Recipients	Amount (mill)	Percent
Inside SMSAs[c]	$1,396.3	79.6%	$3,897.1	85.6%	9,467	$2,476	70.2%
Outside SMSAs	357.1	20.4	654.1	14.4	28,221	1,051	29.8
Total	1,753.4	100.0	4,551.2	100.0	37,688	3,527	100.0

Sources: Total direct federal payments from U.S. Bureau of the Census, *1967 Census of Governments,* vol. 5: *Local Government in Metropolitan Areas,* table 9; and *1972 Census of Governments,* vol. 5: *Local Government in Metropolitan Areas,* table 9. Revenue sharing allocations from Richard P. Nathan et al., *Monitoring Revenue Sharing* (The Brookings Institution, 1975), table 5–6, p. 118.

[a] Includes all local governments receiving funds—counties, municipalities, townships, school districts, and special districts. Does not include revenues of federal origin received by the local governments that were channeled through state governments.

[b] It is assumed that 1971–72 figures for direct federal aid to local governments do not include revenue sharing allocations. Although the 1971–72 fiscal year overlapped with calendar 1972, the first period for which revenue sharing funds were allocated, Census Bureau data collection procedures for fiscal 1972 were underway before the revenue sharing legislation was enacted late in 1972. See U.S. Bureau of Census, *1972 Census of Governments,* vol. 9: *Procedural History,* pp. 41–47. The first revenue sharing checks, applied retroactively to the first half of calendar 1972, were mailed to local governments in December of that year.

[c] Standard metropolitan statistical areas.

fundamental way from the New Federalism policies of decentralization that underlie the general revenue sharing program. Shifting responsibility and power from federal bureaucrats to state and local decision makers has meant the elimination of many of the controls and conditions attached to categorical grants. No government has to apply for general revenue sharing support. Subject only to the constraints of the 1972 formula, the state and local units will continue to receive their entitlement checks regularly through at least the end of 1976, the termination of the first five-year authorization period.

For the smaller local governments in the nation, this is a virtual bonanza. Most have never taken part in the grantsmanship and paper work of the categorical-aid programs that originated in the 1950s and 1960s.[1] They are new participants in the direct federal aid system.

If it brings the small governments and their communities more directly into the federal grant system than before, the New Federalism—as manifested in general revenue sharing—also raises some questions about the nature of their participation. In particular, how much change in traditional policy-making practices is this new infusion of money, responsibility, and power likely to produce? A few commentators see "no strings" and widely distributed aid resulting in an improvement in the policy-making and administrative capacities of small governments by permitting them to attract more expert personnel and helping to fund basic governmental services, such as fire protection and local public works, previously ignored by categorical grants.[2] While I cannot find any writings that maintain general revenue sharing will lead to increased competition for public funds and more citizen participation in governmental budgeting in small communities specifically, this is an assumption more generally applied to the revenue sharing program as a whole by proponents of the New Federalism.[3] A number of writers who are critical about the allocation of nationally raised funds, without requiring their local expenditure according to national priorities, anticipate nothing less than a perpetuation of the status quo in most small communities. The easy money would merely shore up many unviable and unneeded governments, these critics charge, and would actually work as a deterrent to change.[4]

This chapter examines the impacts of the New Federalism on small communities by reviewing some of the findings about the initial revenue sharing decisions at the local level. The research summarized includes a field study of five California counties conducted by the author and two colleagues. More broadly, the chapter is an examination of the role of small governments in American federalism. These governments respond differently than larger and more urban units to shifts in federal–local relations because of differences in local political systems. A central assumption is that traditional policy-making patterns of the small communities are highly resistant to the kinds of externally generated change represented by shifts in federal aid programs.

Why Study Small Governments?

In light of the overriding concern with the problems and political processes of large urban communities, a justification for serious examination of government and politics in smaller places seems in order. There are three good reasons for paying greater attention to the relationship of the small governments to the federal system.

First, the small units and their communities are more significant in the national society than usually assumed. An obvious fact is that there are far more small local governments—and hence small political systems—than larger ones in the country. Not so obvious are the numbers of people governed by these units, depending on the measure of "smallness" used. The following percentages of the nation's population lived in various categories of "small" communities in 1970:[5]

1. 26 percent in rural places and areas
2. 31 percent outside of standard statistical metropolitan areas
3. 42 percent outside of urbanized areas
4. 64 percent outside of cities of more than 50,000 population

Second, the post-World War II growth of the metropolitan areas has slowed in recent years, and smaller communities are beginning to reverse their population losses. In fact, in 1970–73 nonmetropolitan areas grew faster than metropolitan areas—4.2 compared with 2.9 percent—according to a recent Department of Agriculture study.[6] The new trend represents a return to the small town for many core-city and suburban families, but it is a selective trend. Many agriculturally oriented counties, particularly in the Great Plains, continue to lose population. The favored counties contain retirement and recreational towns, cities benefitted by the decentralization of industry, and fringe-area communities within commuting distance of jobs in metropolitan areas.

A third reason for looking closely at small communities is that their problems are intertwined with the problems of the nation's urban areas.[7] The lessening of economic opportunities in rural places that began before World War II, and that was a result of reductions in the number of farms and farmers, directly led to the crowding of the big cities and indirectly brought on the suburban sprawl of metropolitan areas. Some problems such as poverty and inadequate housing are, in fact, proportionately more serious in rural than in urban areas.

The Initial Impact of Revenue Sharing:
A California Study

An intensive field study of local revenue sharing decisions by the author and two colleagues, agricultural economists Varden Fuller and Herbert Mason, suggests that the political impact of this program was greater on large than small local governments.[b] We studied the budgeting of revenue sharing funds by five northern California county governments during 1973 and 1974, the first two appropriation cycles after the funds became available. Two of the counties, although containing extensive agricultural

---

[b] For some of the other findings of this study, see Herbert O. Mason, "Decision Making in Rural Local Government: A Case Study of Revenue Sharing." Ph.D. Dissertation, University of California, Davis, Agricultural Economics, 1975.

and unincorporated areas, are located in standard metropolitan statistical areas. Both have considerably larger populations (about 210,000 and 80,000) than the three nonmetropolitan, essentially rural counties (all under 50,000) in the study.[c]

Table 1-2, summarizing some of the preliminary findings of our research, compares revenue sharing expenditures and budgetary practices in the five counties. Competition for the funds from both county departments and outside groups was greater than elsewhere in the two metropolitan counties, Sonoma and Placer. More emphasis also was given to the conduct of public hearings on the revenue sharing program in these two counties, and their governing boards tended to appropriate proportionately large amounts of such funds on social service purposes including community activities conducted by noncounty agencies.

But only in Placer County, the smaller of these two metropolitan communities, were there substantial changes in budgeting practices and group behavior in 1973-74 as a result of the new revenue sharing program. Here a new arena for competition over county government resources was created. Community groups, noncounty local governments, and county departments besieged the board of supervisors for shares of the revenue sharing pie. Placer County budgeting had never before attracted so much interest and participation. The board responded in 1974 by establishing a special process for soliciting and reviewing funding proposals, which included extensive advertising and the use of citizen commissions for the review of requests for noncounty social service and capital spending. The new procedures were devised after the first round of decisions in 1973, when the board unexpectedly reduced the recommendations of its chief executive for county department capital outlays in order to fund several noncounty social service and special district projects. In effect, the supervisors opened up their budgetary process as a result of constituency pressures.

The effects of revenue sharing on practices in the other four counties were slight or negligible. Three of the other county boards received more group and citizen contacts than during normal budget periods as the result of conducting public hearings. The hearings, however, were conducted more as a means of obtaining public comments on staff and supervisorial plans for spending on county projects than as a method of soliciting outside proposals for noncounty projects. When formally presented, the

---

[c] While Sonoma County is located on the Pacific coast north of San Francisco, the other four counties have inland locations in the Sacramento Valley and Sierra foothill areas. All five county governments are headed by five-member boards of supervisors, elected on nonpartisan ballots from separate districts. Central staffing arrangements vary, with the boards in the three largest counties employing chief executive officers and the other two relying more informally on the assistance of their separately elected county auditors.

Table 1-2
Revenue Sharing Budgeting in Five California Counties, 1973 and 1974[a]

County 1970 Population	Central Staffing for County Board	Total RS Funds Available for Appropriation[a] (Millions)	Percent Capital Improvements[b]	Percent Social Services[c]	Major Functional Purposes
Metropolitan Counties					
Sonoma: 204,885 (separate SMSA)	Appointed CAO[d]	$12.9	96.8%	3.2%	New justice–jail, juv., health bldgs.
Placer: 77,306 (part of Sacramento SMSA)	Appointed CAO[d]	4.2	69.5	12.7	Roads; remodeling; equip.; hospital operations
Nonmetropolitan Counties					
Yuba: 44,736	Appointed CAO[d]	3.4	92.7	.1	Roads and drains; new library
Nevada: 26,346	Elected auditor serving as fiscal director	1.6	31.6	1.0	Roads; remodeling
Glenn: 17,521	Informal staffing by elected auditor	1.3	31.5	.5	Roads; law enforc. salaries

[a] Appropriations made in 1973 and 1974 for spending in 1973–74 and 1974–75 fiscal years, respectively. Included budgeting of revenue sharing funds received or anticipated for first three and one-half years, from calendar 1972 through June 30, 1975.

[b] Many of the expenditures for road work in the three nonmetropolitan counties are classified as operating expenses according to Treasury Department criteria, since they involved augmentations to ongoing repavement ("overly") and repair activities on existing roads, although in a functional sense such work could be considered capital outlay.

[c] For the operating purposes of county welfare departments and/or outside groups.

[d] CAO—"Chief Administrative Officer." Actual titles in individual counties varied.

County	Sources of RS Fund Requests		County Arrangements for Citizen–Group Participation	Characteristics of RS Decision Making	Change from Normal Practices and Politics?
	1973	1974			
Sonoma	County depts.; 6 fire dists.; 11 comm. groups	County depts.; 18 comm. groups	Public hearings in both years	Dominated by CAO recommendations	*Slight:* more group demands on county govt.
Placer	County depts.; 8 spec. dists.; and cities; 12 comm. groups	County depts.; 12 spec. dists.; and cities 17 comm. groups	Public hearing in 1973; elaborate application–review– hearing procedure in 1974	CAO recommendations on county dept. funding accepted; separate decisions by board on noncounty funding	*Considerable:* new budgeting procedures; more group demands
Yuba	No formal requests from county depts.	3 spec. dists.; 2 comm. groups 10 comm. groups	Public hearing only in 1973; informal public contacts by indiv. supervisors	Equal split of most funds among sups.; considerable intra- board conflict; no staff influence	*Slight:* change from countrywide budgeting
Nevada	No procedure for soliciting requests.	1 comm. group	Public Hearing only in 1973	Consensus to spend as much as possible on roads; other recs. of auditor accepted	*None*
Glenn	County depts.; 2 fire dists.; 1 city	County depts.; 2 cities; 3 comm. groups	Public hearings in both years	Board collaboration with select dept. heads—auditor, clerk, engineer	*Slight:* minor increase in group demands

Source: Field and documentary research conducted by Alvin D. Sokolow, Varden Fuller, and Herbert Mason.

requests from community groups generally were brushed aside, as compared to Placer County where the supervisors funded most social service activities proposed by outside groups, about a dozen each year. In one nonmetropolitan county the number of groups requesting funds decreased greatly from 1973 to 1974, after it became clear that the supervisors did not intend to fund social service projects.

What explanations can be offered for the relatively extensive changes in budgeting and group activity in Placer County, and their relative absence in the other four jurisdictions? In Sonoma, largest of the five counties, the board of supervisors long had been faced with a highly fractionalized political environment and the group demands generated by the revenue sharing program were not a new experience. The supervisors did not alter their budgetary practices, by soliciting proposals and outside participation in revenue sharing decisions, largely because of the well-established and dominant role of the county's chief executive officer. They more closely followed staff recommendations than the supervisors of the other counties, which meant an early decision to commit most revenue sharing funds to a few large building projects and a disinclination to tinker with existing budgetary routines. In fact, the supervisors in this largest county were preoccupied with other policy concerns and did not as a governing board pay much direct attention to the revenue sharing program.

The contrast between Placer and the three other counties was more pronounced, and can be explained in terms of already-existing interest group patterns and prior county experiences with federal programs. Larger and more urban than the three nonmetropolitan counties. Placer also in the early 1970s contained a more developed set of organized political interest groups. Supervisors here were accustomed to dealing with a variety of constituency and countywide groups in such nonbudgetary policy areas as land use, environmental protection, water supply, and health care. A community action program (CAP) originally funded by the Office of Economic Opportunity (OEO) contributed to interest group activity. With the reduction in OEO funds, many community action and related groups sought revenue sharing support from the Placer board in 1973–74. Coincidentally, county government officials saw their power to allocate these newly available funds to a variety of purposes as a means of establishing control over CAP activities, a desirable objective in view of alleged mismanagement and excessive overhead in several community action projects. The three nonmetropolitan counties did not have overall community action programs. In general, the supervisors of these rural counties had less experience in dealing with interest group demands and were not prepared to open up their revenue sharing allocation process to outside participants.

Other Early Studies

Several other studies[d] of how local governments handled their first revenue sharing funds in 1973 and 1974 confirm that small and large units responded differently. Differences were noted in the fiscal and political impacts of the general revenue sharing program.

The biggest cities and the largest metropolitan areas obtained the greatest revenue sharing benefits on a per-capita basis under the formula of the 1972 act. But smaller local governments actually obtained proportionately more funds in relation to the income levels of their communities and their local tax efforts.[8] These considerations, combined with the fiscal crises experienced by many of the larger cities in the first half of the 1970s, meant that the smaller governments were more likely to treat their revenue sharing receipts as new and flexible income. The hard-pressed large cities allocated the bulk of their early revenue sharing funds to operating and maintenance purposes, as a substitute for increased taxes and/or service cutbacks, according to the first actual use reports filed with the Treasury Department. Most of these funds went for salaries and other operating purposes. The smaller governments, by comparison, appropriated the majority of their funds for new purposes, primarily for capital improvements. Large governments appropriated greater shares of their revenue sharing funds on social service programs than small governments, although the sums were small compared to the appropriations on public safety and other operating programs.

Rural highway maintenance and construction throughout the United States may have benefitted in 1972–73 by the largest single increment of public funds ever added to this purpose. Almost $200 million was spent on transportation through June 20, 1973 by counties under 250,000 population, the largest revenue sharing expenditure item for these units. In general, the smaller governments—cities, counties, and townships—allocated their first revenue sharing funds for a variety of equipment purchases and construction-remodeling projects. They were able to catch up on deferred maintenance and capital improvement projects. One writer characterized some of these expenditures as "nice-to-have" but not essential.[9]

Reports on the political impacts of revenue sharing are varied, and depend on the research methods employed and the communities studied. The nationwide surveys of the Brookings Institution and the Govern-

---

[d] They include the data compilations of the Treasury Department, the sample survey conducted by the Government Accounting Office (Comptroller General) the first book-length report (Nathan, Manvel, and Calkins, *Monitoring Revenue Sharing*) produced by the Brookings Institution intensive field study of 56 local governments, and studies of local government impacts in the states of Michigan, Wisconsin, Indiana, and California. See 8–11.

ment Accounting Office indicated that citizen and interest group participation in local governmental budgeting increased in about one-third of the sample jurisdictions as a result of the new funds.[10] Paul Terrell cited a considerable broadening of local political processes among California county governments:

General revenue sharing has prompted the use of the traditional local channels of lobbying and petition as well as producing new opportunities for the expression of citizen preferences. In some cases, it has catalyzed innovations in budgeting—innovations chiefly directed to enlarging the scope for citizen input. General revenue sharing has made local politics more important and aroused citizen interest.[11]

Other studies interpreted the increased participation as minimal and disappointing in light of the great anticipations of the New Federalism and questioned the permanent effects on local budgeting and politics.

Generally undisputed, however, is the finding that the political impact of revenue sharing was considerably less in small than large communities.[12] Smaller governments were less inclined to make special arrangements to open the appropriation process to outside involvement. They held relatively few public hearings to solicit ideas and proposals for spending the new federal funds, and they received proportionately fewer demands for a share of the money from interest groups and other nongovernmental sources. Observing that revenue sharing funds were appropriated by local governments in three rural Indiana counties without outside participation, a continuation of conventional budgetary practices, Jon Wendt put the blame on both officials and citizens:

Local units of government have taken no special affirmative action to achieve greater citizen participation and published notices of Revenue Sharing deliberations have been met with citizen apathy. When local residents abrogate their participatory prerogatives they become dependent upon the magnanimity of local officials. Thus legitimate demands may not be expressed and therefore remain unfulfilled resulting in citizen disaffection for governmental service programs that do not meet their needs.[13]

A Model of Small Community Politics

That policy-making practices in small communities were hardly affected by the revenue sharing program would not surprise most political scientists. For more than a half-century small town governments have been damned as inefficient, uneconomical, unresponsive, and unrepresentative. The criticisms may be right, especially from an efficiency point of view, but they seldom have looked beyond the obvious issues of fragmentation and economies of scale.

To understand why small communities are relatively immune to current shifts in federal–local relations, it is important to examine how their local governments and overall political systems operate. Most such communities in the United States appear to contain common characteristics of interest group competition, decision strategies, and administrative styles.[e] Taken together, these characteristics can be said to constitute a model of small community politics, because they are general, interrelated, and have varying applicability to specific communities.

Political systems of small communities contain seemingly contradictory features. On the one hand, politics is a pervasive element of local life. It is the major topic of conversation and rumor; political matters are openly discussed by all and fuel the well-known communications networks of small towns. Face-to-face contacts with public officials occur daily, and local government is both visible and understandable. On the other hand, the political system is usually closed to serious debate of major public issues. Power is tightly held by small and overlapping elites—as compared to the more widespread distribution of power-related resources in larger and more urban places—who are able to prevent the organization of competing interests. People are elected to public office on the basis of personality, length of residence in the locality, and their commitment to the status quo—not because of their proposals for programmatic and policy change.

These two kinds of conditions are not as incompatible as they appear. For elected officials and other decision makers can be accessible to citizens without necessarily being responsive to demands for change.[f] They are skillful at blunting and diverting the demands, at heading them

---

[e] The following generalizations are based on the author's research and observations in a number of small communities in the Midwest and California during the past 15 years, and on the literature of small community politics and government. Case studies and other writings that bear on these generalizations include: Robert E. Agger, Daniel Goldrich, and Bert E. Swanson, *The Rulers and the Ruled: Political Power and Impotence in American Communities* (New York: Macmillan, 1974); Ralph E. Kimbrough, *Political Power and Educational Decision Making* (Chicago: Rand McNally, 1964); Robert Presthus, *Men at the Top: A Study in Community Power* (New York: Oxford University Press, 1964); Warner E. Mills and Harry R. Davis, *Small Community Politics: Seven Cases in Decision Making* (New York: Random House, 1962); Margaret G. Osland, *The Guardians of La Loma* (Indianapolis: Bobbs-Merrill, 1957); Edgar L. Sherbenou, "The Structure and Methods of Political Power in a Small Town," Ph.D. Dissertation, University of Kansas, Political Science, 1956; Arthur S. Vidich and Joseph Bensman, *Small Town in Mass Society: Class, Power, and Religion in a Rural Community* (Princeton: Princeton University Press, 1958); and Evan Z. Vogt, *Modern Homesteaders: The Life of a Twentieth Century Frontier Community* (Cambridge: Harvard University Press, 1955).

[f] Morton Grodzins noted that while citizens of rural areas are relatively close to their local governments, they are not necessarily in control of them. See Grodzins, *The American System: A New View of Government in the United States* (Chicago: Rand McNally, 1966), chapter 7.

off before direct confrontations become necessary. Informality and resistance to change, in fact, are interrelated conditions. They both rest on the traditional need of the small community to avoid serious political conflict. When people know each other very well and in a large variety of social contexts, they are not disposed to openly disagree with each other on public matters. They are fearful of opening up personal animosities that cannot be healed easily. Perhaps such fears are warranted, given the incapacity of institutions in the close-knit community to meditate and absorb serious disagreement. In larger communities the greater neutrality and impersonality of social contacts provide mechanisms for handling conflict.

This desire to avoid serious conflict translates into three types of local political patterns:

1. *The absence of interest-group competition.* A fragile political system cannot tolerate the degree of divisiveness implied by the clash of well-organized interest groups over scarce governmental resources. Governing boards refuse to deal with the leaders of emerging groups, and power elites exercise their economic and social sanctions to discourage organization for political purposes. If dissatisfactions are to be expressed, the proper route is through the community's informal communications network and through the contacts of individual citizens with their accessible public officials. This is not to deny that small communities contain an abundance of organizations—farmers' groups in open-country areas, businessmens' associations in population centers, and everywhere a multiplicity of social, civic, and religious associations. Rarely, however, are such organizations perceived as carrying out local political purposes. On the few occasions that such groups make demands on local government, they are seen as representing general community desires and not as competing with other interests for scarce resources.

2. *Decision strategies that emphasize consensus.* City and village councils, county boards of supervisors, and school boards in small communities apply a variety of strategies to avoid the open expression of conflict. Most of the strategies are implicit and unvoiced, and they include the means by which public meetings are conducted and agenda items are discussed. Governing boards maintain at least a superficial consensus; members voluntarily suppress personal differences over substantive issues for the sake of presenting a united appearance. The effort always is on avoiding direct confrontations with proponents of new policies and programs.

3. *Informal and nonspecialized styles of administration.* Where informality and face-to-face relations mark the operations of local government, the distinction between such separate functions as policy making and routine administration is hard to maintain. Many governing boards spend most of their energies on the details of day-to-day administration, not on

policy deliberation and determination. This is a natural pattern for a small government that lacks full-time employees, let alone an administrative staff. But even when they employ executives or general managers, many city councilmen, county supervisors, and township trustees prefer to intervene in administrative matters. By concentrating on the familiar and the routine, they obtain the satisfaction of carrying out the public's business without having to get involved in the more complicated policy problems that threaten unanimity and the status quo. Informality and limited specialization also characterize the roles and behavior of appointed executives. As administrators, they cannot retreat behind their desks, the budgets they prepare, or the aloofness of their professional values. A premium is placed on their accessibility and friendliness, more so than their expertise. Small city managers and small county executives often are responsible for tasks in many different functional areas,[g] limiting their ability to engage in long-range planning, research, and coordination.

This model of politics, which emphasizes conflict avoidance, is particularly applicable to very small, stable, isolated, and socially homogeneous communities. But even long after communities begin to grow, traditional political conditions endure. Robert Wood found that once-rural communities retained small town political styles long after their suburbanization.[14]

One important consequence of these political patterns is the ability of small communities to resist federal and state government policies that seek to change local practices. Political elites easily coalesce against what they perceive as external threats to local values and traditions. The absence of aggressive administrators and a diversity of political organizations also contribute to a community's united stand.

In general, small community political systems have been more effective than urban systems in opposing externally generated demands, as recent examples from two policy areas illustrate. Small school districts in the South were particularly slow in desegregating their classrooms after the federal court mandates of the 1950s and 1960s.[15] There was a similar pattern in the extent to which districts elsewhere complied with the court decisions of the unconstitutionality of Bible reading and other religion-supporting practices in public schools.[h] Efforts also by state governments

---

[g] The average manager in a city under 10,000 population may serve also as finance director, purchasing agent, city engineer, and building inspector. See David Booth, *Council-Manager Government in Small Cities* (Washington: The International City Management Association, 1968).

[h] Kenneth M. Dolbeare and Phillip E. Hammond, *The School Prayer Decisions: From Court Policy to Local Practice* (Chicago: University of Chicago Press, 1971). Another study found rapid compliance in a rural Illinois community; Richard M. Johnson, *The Dynamics of Compliance: Supreme Court Decision Making from a New Perspective* (Evanston: Northwestern University Press, 1967).

to bring about unwanted shifts in local government operations and structures also encounter stiff opposition in small communities, as seen most prominently in the resistance of thousands of towns to state-required consolidations of their school districts.[i]

The programs of the New Federalism, with the trend away from outside controls, are a different matter. But even programs that offer fiscal advantages to the small community have been known to reinforce local tendencies to preserve the status quo. Arthur S. Vidich and Joseph Bensman made this point in their classic study of the external relations and politics of an upstate New York village and town during the 1950s. While the residents and public officials of Springdale benefitted greatly from state subsidies and policies relating to schools, roads, and other services, they were resentful of the dependence and limited local autonomy implied by the outside aid and accompanying controls. The benefits and dependency provided village and town board members with a rationale for maintaining a caretaker government and denying requests for expanded services. Both the need and the ability to innovate in local government had evaporated with the greater activities and influences of state and national governments. The local decision makers still had the legal capacity to act, but they had lost the psychological capacity to do so— a change termed by Vidich and Bensman as the "political surrender to mass society."[16]

Conclusions: Political Change in the Small Community

There is little prospect that the New Federalism's decentralization of power and responsibility will directly produce significant change in the political and governmental practices of most small communities. The impact has been considerable in a strictly fiscal sense. Revenue sharing funds have given small city and county governments more budgetary maneuverability than the larger urban units. The new, open-ended funds represent relatively large portions of the total revenues now available to the small governments, which also lack the fiscal pressures present in more urban communities. For these reasons, the small units have been able to spend much of their revenue sharing money on capital items, while the hard-pressed large cities have been forced to use the funds on operating programs and tax-reduction purposes. Yet, the enlarged budgetary stakes and enhanced policy-making flexibility have not lead to fundamental changes in local political systems. Increased political

---

[i] For a discussion of school reorganization conflicts, see Alvin D. Sokolow and Vincent Marando, "Rural and Suburban Styles in School District Reorganization: A Study of Two Michigan Districts," Michigan State University, Institute for Community Development and Services (East Lansing: 1971), chapter 1.

participation and competition in the small communities has not occurred on a widespread basis, nor have local governing boards been encouraged to tackle new policy problems and administrative responsibilities.

By itself the decentralization and automatic allocation of federal resources to the small governments cannot insure that these units will change in desired directions. If the objectives are increased public participation in decision processes and greater problem-solving capacities on the part of local officials, the necessary conditions for translating these national goals into local results are much less evident in small than large communities. The smaller political systems generally lack organized and competing interests, elected officials who seek new resources to instigate policy innovations, and influential and aggressive administrators. Prior experiences with the federal categorical-aid programs of the past two decades were too limited to stimulate the development of these conditions. Major shifts in federal–local relations have had little impact on small community political practices.[17] In this sense the small political systems and local governments—although not their communities generally—are relatively isolated from the dynamics of American federalism.

Substantial political change in small communities is more likely to come from internal sources—from ad hoc coalitions of angry citizens who unseat incumbent officials, from newcomer–old timer conflicts that are the natural result of population shifts, and from the accumulation of local policy crises. Only by assaulting the fundamental emphasis on avoiding conflict can the policy and administrative styles of local governments be revised. Such assaults are gradual in their development and impacts, as a number of studies of small town political change have indicated,[18] and they depend initially on the growth of local political organization and competition. Emerging groups can use the opportunities provided by federal grant programs as leverage in challenging traditional practices, but the federal aid by itself is rarely an adequate stimulus for organization and competition.

Notes

1. Richard P. Nathan, Allen D. Manvel, and Susannah E. Calkins, *Monitoring Revenue Sharing* (Washington: The Brookings Institution, 1975), p. 281; and Murray L. Weidenbaum, *Potential Impacts of Revenue Sharing* (Washington: American Enterprise Institute, 1974).

2. Weidenbaum, *Potential Impacts of Revenue Sharing.*

3. David A. Caputo and Richard Cole, *Urban Politics and Decentralization: The Case of General Revenue Sharing* (Lexington: Lexington Books, D.C. Heath and Co., 1974).

4. Michael D. Reagan, "The Pro and Con Arguments," *Annals of the*

American Academy of Political and Social Science, vol. 419 (1975), pp. 23–35. See also, Comptroller General of the United States, *Revenue Sharing and Local Government Modernization* (Washington: Government Accounting Office, April 17, 1975); Michael D. Reagan, *The New Federalism* (New York: Oxford University Press, 1972), chapter 4; Henry S. Reuss, "Should We Abandon Revenue Sharing?" *Annals of the American Academy of Political and Social Science,* vol. 419 (1975), pp. 88–99; and Jay G. Sykes, "Federal Revenue Sharing: The New Boondoggle," *National Civic Review,* vol. 62 (1973), pp. 76–79.

5. U.S. Bureau of the Census, *1970 Census of Population,* vol. 1: "Number of Inhabitants, United States Summary" (Washington: 1971).

6. Calvin L. Beale, *The Revival of Population Growth in Nonmetropolitan America* (Washington: U.S. Department of Agriculture, Economic Research Service, 1975).

7. See Niles M. Hansen, *The Future of Nonmetropolitan America* (Lexington: Lexington Books, D. C. Heath and Co., 1973); and Hansen, *Rural Poverty and the Urban Crisis* (Bloomington: Indiana University Press, 1970).

8. Nathan, Manvel, and Calkins, *Monitoring Revenue Sharing*; Department of the Treasury, *General Revenue Sharing: The First Actual Use Reports* (Washington: March 1, 1974); Comptroller General of the United States, *Revenue Sharing: Its Use by and Impact on Local Governments* (Washington: U.S. Government Accounting Office, April 25, 1974); R. Thomas Martin and Mary S. Patrick, *General Revenue Sharing: The Michigan Experience* (East Lansing: Michigan State University, Center for Rural Manpower and Public Affairs, May 1974); and Wisconsin Department of Local Affairs and Development, *General Revenue Sharing: Its Impact and Use in Wisconsin Localities* (Madison: November 22, 1974).

9. John E. Wendt, *Local Fiscal Assistance: A Report on the Operation of the Federal Revenue Sharing Program in Greene, Martin and Davies Counties, Indiana* (Terre Haute: Indiana State University, The Center for Governmental Services, 1973), p. 7.

10. Nathan, Manvel, and Calkins, *Monitoring Revenue Sharing*; and Comptroller General of the United States, *Revenue Sharing.* See also Caputo and Cole, *Urban Politics,* chapter 5.

11. Paul Terrell, "How Local Governments Involve Citizens in General Revenue Sharing: A California Survey," University of Southern California, Regional Research Institute in Social Welfare (Los Angeles: 1975), p. 20.

12. See Ibid.; Nathan, Manvel, and Calkins, *Monitoring Revenue Sharing*; Martin and Patrick, *General Revenue Sharing*; and Wisconsin Department of Local Affairs and Development, *General Revenue Sharing.*

13. Wendt, *Local Fiscal Assistance,* p. 16.

14. Robert Wood, *Suburbia: Its People and Their Politics* (Boston: Houghton Mifflin, 1958).

15. United States Commission on Civil Rights, *Federal Enforcement of School Desegregation* (Washington: 1969); and Frederick M. Wirt, *Politics of Southern Equality: Law and Social Change in a Mississippi County* (Chicago: Aldine, 1970).

16. Vidich and Bensman, *Small Town in Mass Society,* chapter 4. See also, Roy C. Buck and Robert A. Rath, "Planning as Institutional Innovation in the Smaller City," *American Institute of Planners Journal,* vol. 36 (1970), pp. 59–64; and Don Martindale and R. Galen Hanson, *Small Town and The Nation: The Conflict of Local and Translocal Forces* (Westport: Greenwood Publishing, 1969).

17. Alvin D. Sokolow, "Small Community Policy Making and the New Federalism," paper presented at the American Political Science Association 1975 Annual Meeting, San Francisco, Calif., September 4, 1975.

18. Robert Aguallo, Jr., and Adaljiza Sosa Riddell, "Local Politics, Local Elites, and Political Change: The Case of Parlier, California," paper presented to the Annual Meeting of the Western Political Science Association, Seattle, 1975; William M. Dobriner, "The Natural History of a Reluctant Suburb," *The Yale Review,* vol. 49 (1960), pp. 399–412; John Staples Shockley, *Chicano Revolt in a Texas Town* (Notre Dame: University of Notre Dame Press, 1974); Alvin D. Sokolow, *Governmental Response to Urbanization: Three Townships on the Rural-Urban Gradient* (Washington: United States Department of Agriculture, Economic Research Service, 1968); Christopher Sower, John Holland, Kenneth Tiedke, and Walter Freeman, *Community Involvement: The Ties that Make for Action* (Glencoe: The Free Press, 1957); and Frederick M. Wirt, Benjamin Walter, Francine F. Rabinowitz, and Deborah R. Hensler, *On the City's Rim: Politics and Policy in Suburbia* (Lexington: D. C. Heath and Co., 1972), Chapter 12.

2

Patterns of Revenue Sharing Expenditure from the Actual Use Reports

Richard A. Smith and David Cozad

A growing body of literature has been developing over the past decade on the conditions under which communities are likely to adopt particular types of policies and programs. Various policies have been the subject of these analyses, including urban renewal, public housing, poverty programs, flouridation, school desegregation, and others, in an attempt to discern the social, economic, and political conditions associated with successful adoption and implementation. One particularly strong finding from these studies is that the abilities of communities to respond to federally designed programs and extra-community policy initiatives is not evenly distributed; some communities are more likely to adopt and implement successfully certain types of programs than others. These differential capacities appear to be associated with various social and political conditions of the communities concerned.

These community policy studies, in clarifying these differential abilities, have lead to the the common observation that many federal programs, designed for the average but abstract community, may not be readily adapted to local community conditions. In the abstract, many programs may appear to be well designed, efficacious responses to particular problems, but within the various local environments within which they must be made workable, they may be inappropriate. The "best" program, in a causal sense, may not be the best given the preference, priorities, organizational capacities, and unique set of problems and circumstances of a local community.

One means of adapting programs better to local requirements may be through both general and special block grants to cities whereby local governments can expend funds on the particular set of programs and projects that it believes appropriate in light of its problems and needs. The passage of general revenue sharing legislation in 1972 was based somewhat on these observations. Thus, block grants are given to local governments, allowing them to allocate this money to a wide variety of program areas according to locally perceived needs, and it is believed that this is likely to result in more responsive local governments and a better matching of funds with requirements.

21

Given this flexibility for allocating funds and prior indications that community policy decisions tend to be related to various social and political characteristics of communities (Aiken 1970; Clark 1968; Crain, Katz, and Rosenthal 1969; Hawley 1963), we would expect significant differences to exist in the patterns by which particular types of communities spend their revenue sharing funds. Should such differences not exist, then the argument that local conditions affect policy outputs would not hold for revenue sharing decisions, and one (although by no means all) arguments for instituting and maintaining revenue sharing would be diminished. Some initial indications of this variability do exist. David Caputo and Richard Cole (1973), in data collected through a survey of 212 cities, show that differences in allocations to various categories occur by city size, region, metropolitan status, and type of municipal government. Such differences, however, were small and limited to a few expenditure categories. Most cities, regardless of characteristics, spent the largest proportion of their funds in a relatively few expenditure categories and, overall, similarities rather than differences in spending patterns were observed.

A further investigation of these differences seems warranted and has now been made possible by the availability of new data from the Office of Revenue Sharing, U.S. Department of the Treasury. These data reflect the actual expenditures as reported by each local community. The present study will use these Actual Use Reports for 376 cities, distinguished on the basis of political, social, and ecological variables, in an effort to investigate further patterned variations in revenue expenditures. Specifically, we will address the following three questions:

1. Do cities of different political characteristics distribute their revenue sharing funds differently across the various expenditure categories?
2. Within any one expenditure category, do cities with different political characteristics allocate differing amounts of their revenue sharing funds?
3. Within any one expenditure category, do the social and ecological conditions of communities, in conjunction with its political characteristics, affect revenue sharing allocations?

Data and Method

The Actual Use Reports available at the time of this analysis covered expenditures for the first six-month period of the revenue sharing program, from January 1 through June 30, 1973. Since the program, when passed in October 1972, was made retroactive to January 1, 1972, the money available to local communities by June 1973 represented almost one and one-half years of funds. Actual expenditures are reported by local communities in two broad classifications, operating–maintenance expenditures and capital expenditures, each of which is further subdivided into a number of general expenditure categories. Thirteen such general expenditure categories are identified, as follows: public safety, environmental protection–conservation, public transportation, health–hospitals, recreation–culture, libraries, social services for the poor and aged, financial administration, and education (see Caputo and Cole 1974 for examples of the types of programs included within each category). In addition to these 13 expenditure categories the use reports also include an "other" category for projects not subsumed under existing headings. Only in this other category are specific projects enumerated, so that generally, the particular projects funded by a city and included under each expenditure category are unknown.

Since our focus is on the expenditure categories, the distinctions by the broad classifications of operating–maintenance and capital expenditures were not maintained, and expenditures in categories appearing under both classifications were aggregated. A few other expenditure categories were combined, as follows: recreation and culture with libraries; social services with social development; financial administration with multipurpose, general government; economic development with housing and community development, yielding a total of nine expenditure categories. Last, specific projects noted in the "other" category were reallocated to one of these nine categories according to the guidelines in Caputo and Cole (1974). In the great majority of instances no ambiguities occurred and we saw no reason why many of these projects were originally allocated to this residual category. We suspect that many cities may have had some difficulty in using the guidelines and if this is true then there are likely to be other misallocations that are unknown.

Our dependent variable is measured as the percentage of total revenue sharing funds allocated to each of the nine expenditure categories. Within the variable of total revenue sharing funds was included both funds received through the program as of June 30, 1973 and accumulated interest on that money, that is, total funds available.

Our purpose is to analyze these allocations by various political, social, and ecological characteristics of communities. As political characteristics we have selected the standard variables measuring reformed and nonreformed governments, along with a composit index of reformism based on the number of reform attributes within any community. These variables are as follows (data source: International City Managers Association 1967–1968):

1. Form of Government: mayor, manager-council
2. Type of elections: partisan, nonpartisan

3. Type of representation: ward, mixed, at large
4. Index of reform: 0–3, according to number of reformed attributes

Six variables are included as measures of the social and ecological characteristics of communities, as follows (data source: U.S. Bureau of the Census 1972):

1. Ecological status: central city, suburb
2. Region: North, South, Midwest, West
3. Size: over 500,000 population; 250,000–500,000; 100,000–250,000; 50,000–100,000.
4. Black population: high (one-third of cities with highest percentage of black population, ≥ 14.3%); medium (middle one-third of cities, 3.2–14.1%); low (one-third of cities with lowest percentage, ≤ 3.1%)
5. Ethnic composition: high (one-third of cities with highest percentage of foreign born and first generation, ≥ 24%); medium (middle one-third of cities, 11.9–23.9%); low (bottom one-third of cities, ≤ 11.8%)
6. Median family income: high (above $10,000 in East and South, above $11,000 in Midwest and West); medium ($9,000–10,000 in East, $8,000–10,000 in South, $10,000–11,000 in Midwest and West); low (below $9,000 in East, below $8,000 in South, below $10,000 in West and Midwest).

The sample size of 376 cities represents all incorporated places of over 50,000 population (1970) with the exception of 19 for which complete data were not available. Since the analysis compares only mayor and manager forms for government, omitting commission types, the sample size drops to 352 when form of government and the index of reform are considered.

Analysis

Total Expenditures

Since our data refer to only allocations made during the first six months of the revenue sharing program, it is possible that many cities were not able to formulate plans for expending their funds within this short span of time, thereby resulting in a large percentage of cities spending little or no revenue sharing money. To test this possiblity we have computed the appropriate frequencies for cities spending none, less than 5 percent and more than 75 percent of their funds, as shown in table 2–1. The average level of expenditure by all cities was 45.7 percent, a figure that we do not regard as exceedingly high. While only a small percentage of cities spent none of their funds, and a reasonably large percentage spent over 75 percent, the total amount of funds remaining unaccounted for is still considerable, and further allocations by the cities in the latter half of 1973 may prove any patterns found herein invalid. In an effort to reduce these possibilities an initial analysis was undertaken with a smaller sample, eliminating all cities that had spent less than 10 percent of their funds. This analysis showed that although the average levels of expenditures in each category were increased, the overall pattern was substantially the same as found in the larger sample and reported here. We therefore

Table 2–1
Percentage of Total Funds Expended by Political Characteristics

	Percentage Spent		
	None	*< 5%*	*> 75%*
All cities	10.4	19.7	29.5
Government			
Mayor	10.5	19.1	35.5
Manager	11.0	21.0	24.5
Elections			
Partisan	13.4	18.1	30.7
Nonpartisan	8.8	20.2	24.5
Representation			
Ward	10.1	17.4	34.8
Mixed	4.2	13.9	38.9
At large	12.3	2.1	25.1
Index of reform			
0 attributes	13.1	21.3	36.1
1 attribute	5.4	10.8	36.5
2 attributes	13.1	21.4	32.1
3 attributes	10.2	22.3	22.3

approach our analysis with some assurances but also with a reasonable degree of caution.

Table 2–1 also shows the distribution of funds expended by political characteristics. Two points are worth noting. First, communities with mixed forms of representation and containing only one reform attribute are substantially underrepresented in cities spending none or less than 5 percent of their funds. Second, nonreformed communities and those with less than two reformed attributes, are substantially overrepresented in the group of cities spending a high proportion of their money. We cannot offer an explanation as to why these mixed or combination systems may be less likely to be slow in entering the program; perhaps the particular combination of reformed and nonreformed attributes is particularly functional for promoting swift action. The latter pattern, showing nonreformed systems more likely to spend a higher proportion of their money more swiftly, does find some correspondence in the literature. David J. Greenstone and Paul E. Peterson (1968) have argued that reformed and nonreformed governments have different styles, with the latter more disposed to obtaining and dispensing funds quickly while the former may be more concerned with organizing communitywide inputs for formulating action plans. Caputo and Cole's data (1973) lend this argument some further support by reporting that reformed governments were much more likely to use public hearings in conjunction with revenue sharing decisions, and that nonreformed governments had allocated a substantially higher percentage of their total funds than the reformed types.

Expenditure Patterns Across Categories

What is the pattern of allocations to the nine expenditure categories and do cities of different political characteristics tend to allocate their funds in dissimilar ways? The data reported in table 2–2 show the mean percentage expenditure by cities in each of these nine expenditure areas. These data reveal that substantial similarities exist in the ranking of categories by allocations to them, but that within these overall similarities, significant differences in percentage allocations exist

For all cities, the single greatest area of expenditure is public safety. Allocations to the categories of transportation, recreation and culture, environment, and general government closely approximate each other and fall markedly below allocations to safety. Allocations to the remaining areas of health, economic development and housing, social services and development, and education are the least. The overall pattern of differences in these nine allocations is statistically significant at or below the 0.05 level.

While changes in the percentages occur when cities are considered according to political attributes, the overall pattern of allocations is similar; expenditures for public safety always rank first, followed by the two broad groups noted above. But while these overall patterns remain consistent, marked differences in the expenditures for many categories occur. For example, mayor governments are shown to spend considerably more than manager types for safety, while the latter spend more for recreation and culture. Similar differences exist throughout table 2–2 suggesting that the political characteristics of a community may be closely associated with levels of expenditures within particular expenditure areas.

Table 2-2
Percent of Revenue Sharing Funds Allocated by Cities to Each of Nine Expenditure Categories (Rank Order of Expenditures Given in Parentheses)

	Safety	Transp.	Rel/Cul	Envir.	Gen. Gov.	Health	Ecol/Hsg	Social	Educ.	Significance
					Expenditure Categories					
All cities	21.8(1)	6.1(2)	5.4(3)	5.2(4)	4.0(5)	1.4(6)	0.8(7.5)	0.8(7.5)	0.2(9)	*
Government										
Mayor	29.3(1)	7.0(2)	3.9(4)	6.2(3)	3.2(5)	1.1(6)	0.6(7)	0.5(8)	0.2(9)	*
Manager	15.9(1)	5.4(3)	6.9(2)	4.4(5)	4.6(4)	1.5(6)	0.8(8)	1.1(7)	0.1(9)	*
Elections										
Partisan	26.9(1)	7.0(2)	3.2(5)	4.1(4)	4.6(3)	1.5(6)	0.6(8)	0.9(7)	0.1(8)	*
Nonpartisan	19.1(1)	5.7(3.5)	6.6(2)	5.7(3.5)	3.7(5)	1.4(6)	1.0(7)	0.8(8)	0.2(9)	*
Representation										
Ward	28.3(1)	5.7(3)	3.0(5)	7.6(2)	3.5(4)	1.0(7)	0.1(8)	1.4(6)	0.0(9)	*
Mixed	29.5(1)	9.0(2)	5.2(4)	5.5(3)	4.1(5)	2.0(6)	0.7(7)	0.6(8)	0.1(9)	*
At large	17.5(1)	5.4(3)	6.3(2)	4.4(4)	4.1(5)	1.3(6)	1.1(7)	0.7(8)	0.2(9)	*
Index of reformism										
0	27.5(1)	7.4(2)	3.9(5)	4.7(3)	4.0(4)	1.5(6)	0.2(8)	0.5(7)	0.1(9)	*
1	32.7(1)	7.7(2)	2.7(5)	7.2(3)	3.2(4)	1.3(6)	0.8(8)	1.1(7)	0.03(9)	*
2	20.4(1)	5.9(2)	5.6(3)	5.1(4)	4.6(5)	1.7(6)	0.7(8)	0.9(7)	0.3(9)	*
3	14.3(1)	5.0(3)	7.8(2)	4.5(4)	4.0(5)	1.3(6)	1.2(7)	0.8(8)	0.2(9)	*

Note: Asterisk (*) used to denote statistically significant relationships at or below the 0.05 level, as computed by a one-way analysis of variance.

Expenditures within Categories

The data shown in tables 2–3 to 2–8 represent mean percentage allocations within each of the expenditure areas considered separately and organized according to both the political characteristics of communities and selected social–ecological characteristics. Given the high volume of data that these analyses have produced we have chosen to include tables only for those categories showing some pattern in expenditures, and within each table we have reported only those relationships showing statistical significance at or below the 0.05 level. The advantage of this latter selectivity is that it shows immediately the important patterns that may exist. Each of these tables should be read in both the horizontal and vertical directions. Where data are entered horizontally the relevant research question is, "Do cities of a given social–ecological type show significant differences in allocations according to characteristics of their political systems?" Where data are entered vertically the research question is, "Do cities of a particular political type vary in their allocations according to their social–ecological characteristics?" The first question tests for relationships among political systems while holding social and ecological characteristics constant; the latter question holds political characteristics constant to test for the effects of social and ecological characteristics.

Public Safety: Table 2–3 shows a high proportion of statistically significant differences in expenditures for public safety for cities with different political characteristics. For all cities, the various nonreformed types of systems show higher levels of expenditure than their reformed counterparts. These general relationships are maintained in most instances when controls for social and ecological characteristics are introduced.

One important exception to these relationships involves the control for region. When applied, all of these significant differences disappear, providing strong indications that while types of political systems may differentiate between expenditures nationally, cities within any region may be relatively homogeneous in their safety expenditures. The importance of region is reaffirmed when type of political system is controlled (vertical relationships) in an attempt to examine distinctions by social and ecological characteristics. The data indicate that in almost every instance significant differences exist between regions. Thus, for example, mayor governments in the East are shown to spend considerably more on safety than mayor governments in the West, but that mayor and manager governments in both regions are similar to each other in the percentages allocated. These same patterns exist for elections, representation, and the index of reform, indicating a substantial degree of intraregional homogeneity and interregional heterogeneity in expenditures.

While intraregional homogeneity appears to exist generally, it is still possible that under particular social and ecological conditions types of political systems will serve to differentiate between levels of expenditure within each region. In order to investigate these internal regional patterns the analysis was repeated by region, that is, only those cities within each region were included in each of four separate analyses. The results of this analysis showed that few intraregional patterns exist.

Transportation: The data on transportation expenditures, shown in table 2-4, provide little evidence that the political characteristics of communities affect allocations to this area. More so than political characteristics, various social and ecological conditions appear to be important, particularly for reformed type cities. Thus, while no difference in expenditures is found for nonreformed cities in central cities and suburbs, reformed governments consistently spend more for transportation in central cities than in suburbs. Income and ethnicity are also shown to be important conditions, with the highest levels of transportation expenditures generally occurring in cities with low median incomes and low levels of ethnicity. Expenditures are also highest in the South and Midwest.

As with public safety, region is shown to be an important condition affecting expenditures, and the pattern of intraregional homogeneity and interregional heterogeneity is in evidence. Under particular social and ecological conditions, however, intraregional homogeneity is less apparent for Midwest; the separate regional analysis showed that in suburban cities, cities with 50,000–100,000 population, and those with high income and low to medium percentages of black population, nonreformed types of political systems have higher levels of expenditure than their reformed counterparts.

Recreation and Culture: The data shown in table 2-5 suggest that political systems may be important factors affecting recreation and culture expenditures for particular types of communities: in suburban cities, in those with population of 50,000–100,000, in those with a low percentage of black population, median ethnicity, high median income, and in the South and the West. In each instance reformed governments allocate higher percentages of revenue sharing funds than nonreformed systems. These relationships are also most likely to occur in the South and West and among cities of high median family income. The importance of suburban status is reaffirmed in the vertical relationships: reformed

Table 2-3
Expenditures for Safety by Political, Social, and Ecological Characteristics

	Government		Elections			Representation		Reform Index			
	Mayor	Mgr.–Cncl.	Partisan	Nonpart.	Ward	Mixed	At Large	0	1	2	3
All cities	29.3	15.9 *	26.9	19.1 *	28.3	29.5	17.5 *	27.5	32.7	20.4	14.3 *
Metro. status											
Central city	28.6	16.2 *	—	—	26.4	30.7	18.5 *	27.8	28.1	21.9	15.5 *
Suburb	31.6	15.5 *	32.9	16.7 *	34.8	25.2	15.8 *	26.1	46.6	17.5	12.9 *
Size											
Over 500,000	37.2	8.6 *	48.9	18.2 *	—	—	—	50.8	26.1	28.2	9.3 *
250–500,000	—	—	—	—	—	—	—	—	—	—	—
100–250,000	—	—	23.9	14.9 *	—	—	—	—	—	—	—
50–100,000	31.3	16.1 *	—	—	29.4	29.5	17.3 *	24.4	36.5	19.7	15.2 *
	*	*	*	*		*	*	*	*	*	*
Region											
East	43.0	34.4	38.7	44.0	—	50.8	35.6	40.4	40.9	40.0	40.6
South	14.3	10.2	11.6	12.4	—	9.3	12.2	4.6	16.3	12.6	10.1
Midwest	24.2	23.4	23.0	24.5	—	20.2	22.6	19.7	35.3	16.2	24.2
West	11.2	11.9	16.3	11.6	—	4.4	11.3	3.3	10.2	21.3	9.8
	*	*	*	*		*	*	*	*	*	*
Income											
High	25.3	14.2 *	30.4	14.0 *	—	—	16.7 *	24.9	36.3	12.1	11.8 *
Medium	34.5	16.5 *	—	—	39.4	30.9	—	31.4	30.1	30.8	12.9 *
Low	28.0	17.4 *	—	—	—	—	—	—	—	16.2	—
										*	
Ethnicity											
High	—	24.5 *	35.7	28.9	28.9	44.3	23.3 *	—	—	—	21.4 *
Medium	31.4	10.9 *	25.3	—	—	19.2	—	25.2	35.1	15.7	10.6 *
Low	—	14.6	18.8	—	—	19.8	—	—	—	—	12.5
		*	*			*					*

Black											
High	31.3	19.4 *	—	17.8 *	—	—	16.4 *	—	—	27.0	—
Medium	29.8	16.4 *	28.5	—	30.0	28.2	13.9 *	25.0	37.9	28.5	11.5 *
Low	27.4	12.3 *	—		26.5	28.4		26.5	33.8	7.2 *	14.7 *

Note: The direction of statistically significant relationships (at or below 0.05 level) is indicated by an asterisk (*) in the horizontal and vertical dimensions. All relationships are computed by a one-way analysis of variance.

Table 2–4
Expenditures for Transportation by Political, Social, and Ecological Characteristics

	Government		Elections			Representation			Reform Index			
	Mayor	Mgr.-Cncl.	Partisan	Nonpart.	Ward	Mixed	At Large	0	1	2	3
All cities					5.7	9.0	5.4 *				
Metro. status											
Central city	—	7.9	—	7.5	—	—	7.1	—	—	—	7.4
Suburb	—	2.3 *	—	2.9 *	—	—	2.3 *	—	—	—	2.2 *
Size											
Over 500,000											
250–500,000											
100–250,000											
50–100,000											
Region											
East	4.1	5.2	4.6	3.9	—	—	2.6	—	—	—	0.2
South	7.3	9.0	7.7	9.0	—	—	8.6	—	—	—	8.7
Midwest	10.8	5.9	11.0	7.2	—	—	6.3	—	—	—	6.6
West	3.7 *	2.6 *	2.3 *	2.7 *	—	—	2.8 *	—	—	—	2.5 *
Income											
High	—	2.0	2.3	3.0 *	—	2.9	2.4	—	—	—	
Medium	—	6.4	9.6	5.1	—	9.6	6.2	—	—	—	
Low	—	8.7 *	8.0 *	9.1 *	—	14.4 *	7.5 *	—	—	—	
Ethnicity											
High	5.5	1.7 *	—	3.1	3.6	7.5	2.4				
Medium	4.7	5.1	—	4.7	—	—	4.4				
Low	11.7 *	8.5 *	—	9.4 *	—	—	8.6 *				

Black						
High	—	—	6.0	—	—	2.3
Medium	—	—	2.5	—	—	5.8
Low	5.9	7.2	7.4 *	*	—	8.1
			*			*

Note: The direction of statistically significant relationships (at or below 0.05 level) is indicated by an asterisk (*) in the horizontal and vertical dimensions. All relationships are computed by a one-way analysis of variance.

systems consistently spend more for recreation and culture in suburbs than in central cities. While region is not shown to be a particularly important variable in this instance, the general pattern of relationships shown in table 2–5 do not hold on an intraregional basis.

Environment: The analysis of environmental expenditures (not reported) showed few relationships with both political and social–ecological variables. The most consistent of these relationships exists by region for reformed governments, indicating significant interregional heterogeneity. These expenditures were also lowest in the West for all measures of reformed government, but no other consistent ranking of the regions was in evidence. No firm generalization appeared on an intraregional basis.

General Government Expenses: Very few significant differences in allocations occurred for this expenditure category (not reported) and no patterns were discernable either by political characteristics or social–ecological variables. Intraregional relationships also were nonexistent.

Health: While expenditures for health are not significantly distinguished by political characteristics generally, such distinctions do occur in particular types of cities (table 2–6): suburbs, cities with 50,000–100,000 population, high medium income, a low percentage of black population and in the West. In each case nonreformed communities allocate higher percentages of their funds than reformed cities.

Particular types of social and ecological characteristics also appear to be important in distinguishing between levels of health expenditures. Region is generally important and in reformed cities, the highest level of expenditure is made by medium income cities.

Intraregionally, the greater level of expenditure made by nonreformed cities in the West is maintained under a variety of social and ecological conditions: in central cities, those with 50,000–100,000 population and those with low median income and a low percentage of black population.

Economic Development and Housing: Table 2–7 shows only a few significant differences in allocations to this category, most of which are maintained by the ward/at-large distinction, with higher expenditures occurring in the latter. None of the social and ecological variables show any consistent relationships to expenditures for particular types of political systems. The intraregional analysis also failed to show evidence of any marked regional patterns.

Social Services and Development: A small number of significant relationships are shown in table 2–8, most of which indicate higher levels of expenditure for cities with various reformed attributes, but mostly as distinguished by form of government. Similarly, only a few significant differences occur within particular political attributes by social and ecological characteristics. Generally, social expenditures are shown to be higher in central cities, in those of medium income and those with a high percentage of black population when such cities also have selected reformed characteristics.

While no regional patterns are shown above, the more detailed intraregional analysis showed reasonably strong patterns in the East and Midwest. In both instances cities with various reformed characteristics displayed higher levels of expenditures, particularly in instances of central cities, 100,000–250,000 population, low to medium levels of income and medium to high percentages of black population.

Education: Virtually no significant differences in expenditures for education exist, both nationally and on an intraregional basis.

Summary Patterns

It is clear from the preceding analysis that a number of generalized patterns in revenue sharing expenditures do occur. We shall review these major patterns; details can be gleaned from the separate tables.

The data show that type of political system does not universally affect revenue sharing allocations. Significant differences in expenditures between the various reformed and nonreformed attributes occur most generally in only two expenditure categories, public safety and recreation–culture, and less consistently in the other areas of health, economic development–housing, and social services and development. For each of these five categories no one type of political system is consistently associated with higher level of expenditures. Rather, nonreformed cities show higher expenditures on safety and health, while reformed governments tend to spend more than nonreformed types in the recreation–culture, economic development–housing and social areas. While it is tempting to suggest some overall pattern to these expenditures by type of political system, such as in following Lewis A. Froman's (1967) distinction between areal and segmental policies, no such suggestions are possible. Each of these expenditure categories is likely to incorporate a wide variety of specific programs so that within any one category both areal and segmental, fragile and nonfragile (Clark 1968), etc., programs will exist.

Table 2-5
Expenditures for Recreation and Culture by Political, Social, and Ecological Characteristics

	Government		Elections		Representation			Reform Index			
	Mayor	Mgr.–Cncl.	Partisan	Nonpart.	Ward	Mixed	At Large	0	1	2	3
All cities	3.9	6.9 *	3.2	6.6 *	3.0	—	6.3 *	3.9	2.7	5.6	7.8 *
Metro status											
Central city	3.5	4.6	—	4.6	—	—	4.5	—	—	—	5.1
Suburb	—	9.9 *	1.8	9.7 *	—	—	9.2 *	2.3	—	—	10.8 *
Size											
Over 500,000	—	—	—	—	—	—	—	—	—	—	—
250–500,000	—	—	—	—	9.0	—	5.6 *	—	—	—	—
100–250,000	—	—	—	—	2.8	—	6.2 *	—	—	—	—
50–100,000	3.5	7.3 *	2.4	7.2 *	3.1	—	6.5 *	2.9	—	—	8.1 *
Region											
East	—	—	—	1.4	—	1.9	—	—	—	—	—
South	—	—	—	7.1	2.0	5.6	6.1 *	—	—	—	5.9 *
Midwest	—	—	—	4.6	—	4.7	—	1.6	—	—	—
West	1.5	10.3 *	—	9.6 *	—	25.4 *	—	1.8	—	—	10.4 *
Income											
High	2.7	9.5 *	—	—	—	—	—	3.0	—	—	10.2 *
Medium	—	—	—	—	—	—	—	—	—	—	—
Low	—	—	—	—	—	—	—	1.8	—	—	5.1 *
Ethnicity											
High	3.6	8.4 *	—	—	—	1.6	5.9 *	—	—	—	—
Medium	—	—	—	—	1.6	10.9	—	—	—	—	—
Low	—	—	—	—	—	5.0 *	—	—	—	—	—

Black					
High	—	—	—	—	—	—
Medium	—	—	—	—	—	—
Low	3.6	10.0 *	1.9	8.7 *	2.0	10.4 *

Note: The direction of statistically significant relationships (at or below 0.05 level) is indicated by an asterisk (*) in the horizontal and vertical dimensions. All relationships are computed by a one-way analysis of variance.

Table 2–6
Expenditures for Health by Political, Social, and Ecological Characteristics

	Government		Elections			Representation		Reform Index			
	Mayor	Mgr.–Cncl.	Partisan	Nonpart.	Ward	Mixed	At Large	0	1	2	3
All cities											
Metro. status											
Central city	—	2.6	—	2.0							
Suburb	0.8	0.2 *	—	3.7 *				0.4	1.4	0.1	0.2 *
Size											
Over 500,000						—	—	—	—		1.4
250–500,000						—	—	—	—		0.5
100–250,000					1.1	—	—	—	—		4.4
50–100,000						2.7	0.6 *	1.2			0.1 *
Region											
East	—	0.6	—	1.1	—	0.9	0.9				
South	0.8	4.6 *	—	3.5	—	8.5	3.1				
Midwest	1.3	0.4	—	1.1	—	1.3	0.9				
West	1.2	0.1 *	1.1	0.1 *	—	0.2	0.1	3.4	0.02	0.3	0.1 *
Income											
High	1.0	0.1 *	—	0.5			0.3	1.2	1.0	0.2	0.1 *
Medium	—	3.5	—	3.0		—	3.2				3.3
Low	—	1.0 *	—	0.7 *		—	0.7 *				0.6 *
Ethnicity											
High	1.0	0.2 *									
Medium	—	0.9									
Low	—	3.2 *									

Black
High —
Medium —
Low 1.5

3.6
1.1
0.1 *
*

—
—
1.6

—
—
1.1

—
—
0.2 *

—
—
1.8

—
—
1.5

—
—
0.4

—
—
0.1 *

Note: The direction of statistically significant relationships (at or below 0.05 level) is indicated by an asterisk (*) in the horizontal and vertical dimensions. All relationships are computed by a one-way analysis of variance.

Table 2-7
Expenditures for Economic Development by Political, Social, and Ecological Characteristics

| | Government | | Elections | | Representation | | | Reform Index | | | |
	Mayor	Mgr.–Cncl.	Partisan	Nonpart.	Ward	Mixed	At Large	0	1	2	3
All cities					0.1	—	1.1 *		—	—	—
Metro. status											
Central city					0.1	—	1.3 *		—	—	—
Suburb					—	—	—		—	—	—
Size											
Over 500,000					—	—	—	—	—	—	—
250–500,000					—	—	—	—	—	—	—
100–250,000					—	—	—	—	—	—	—
50–100,000					0.1	—	1.3 *	0.0	—	—	0.9 *
Region											
East			—	0.4	—	0.4	—	0.0	—	—	—
South			—	0.7	—	1.4	—	23.0	—	—	—
Midwest			—	0.2	—	0.01	—	0.0	—	—	—
West			—	2.0 *	—	4.8 *	—	0.0 *	—	—	1.5 *
Income											
High					—	0.0	—		—	—	—
Medium					—	0.0	—		—	—	—
Low					0.1	2.2 *	1.3 *		—	—	—
Ethnicity											
High	—	—			—	—	—		—	—	—
Medium	0.1	0.8 *			0.1	—	1.3 *		—	—	—
Low	—	—			—	—	—		—	—	—

Black
High
Medium
Low

0.3	—	1.7 *	—	—
—	—	0.0	—	1.3 *
—	—	—	—	—

Note: The direction of statistically significant relationships (at or below 0.05 level) is indicated by an asterisk (*) in the horizontal and vertical dimensions. All relationships are computed by a one-way analysis of variance.

Table 2-8
Expenditures for Social by Political, Social, and Ecological Characteristics

	Government		Elections		Representation			Reform Index			
	Mayor	Mgr.–Cncl.	Partisan	Nonpart.	Ward	Mixed	At Large	0	1	2	3
All cities											
Metro. status											
Central city	0.6	1.6 *	—	1.1							
Suburb	—	0.3 *	—	0.3 *							
Size											
Over 500,000	1.4	—			—	1.5	—	0.6			
250–500,000	0.9	—			—	1.8	—	4.5			
100–250,000	0.2	—			—	0.01	—	0.3			
50–100,000	0.2 *	—			—	0.4 *	—	0.3 *			
Region											
East											
South											
Midwest											
West											
Income											
High	—	—	—	0.1	—	—	0.2	—	—	—	0.1
Medium	0.5	1.8 *	—	1.4	—	—	1.6	—	—	—	1.7
Low	—	—	—	0.8 *	—	—	0.5 *	—	—	—	0.4 *
Ethnicity											
High	—	—			—	—	—				
Medium	0.2 *	1.1 *			2.9	0.2	0.4 *				
Low	—	—			—	—	—				

Black									
High	1.6	5.1 *	0.2	—	1.4 *	—	—	—	1.8
Medium	—	—	3.5	0.1	0.5 *	0.2	3.4	0.5	0.3 *
Low	—	—	—	—	0.3 *	—	—	—	0.2 *

Note: The direction of statistically significant relationships (at or below 0.05 level) is indicated by an asterisk (*) in the horizontal and vertical dimensions. All relationships are computed by a one-way analysis of variance.

While significant differences in percentage allocations do exist in each of these five categories, the magnitude of these differences frequently is small. Only in the case of public safety do reformed and nonreformed governments spend markedly different percentages of their total allocations (differences average about 10%) so as to suggest distinct policy orientations. For recreation–culture, the differences average about 3 percent, and about 1 percent for the remaining three areas. The latter do not really suggest differences between types of political systems that are of any real importance.

The pattern of relationships is made even more complex by accounting for the various social and ecological conditions under which the separate political attributes do distinguish between levels of expenditure. In the great majority of instances, political characteristics are associated with expenditure differentials only in particular types of communities. In addition to *nonreformed* systems spending more for *public safety* under most social and ecological conditions, the following other relationships appear in tables 2–2 to 2–8:

1. *Reformed* governments spend more on *recreation–culture* under the conditions of: suburbs, 50,000–100,000 population, high median income, median levels of ethnicity, low percentage of black population, and in the South and West.
2. *Nonreformed* governments spend more on *health* under the conditions of: suburbs, 50,000–100,000 population, high median income, low percentage of black population and in the West.
3. *Reformed* governments spend more on *economic development–housing* under the conditions of 50,000–100,000 population, low median income, medium levels of ethnicity and medium percentages of black population.
4. *Reformed* governments spend more on *social services and development* under the conditions of: medium income, high levels of black population, and in central cities.

While no particular generalizations are possible concerning the social and ecological conditions under which the different types of political systems tend to affect expenditure levels, the above relationships do show both some patterns and contradictions in terms of the purported styles of the two political systems. (e.g., see Lineberry and Fowler 1967; Banfield 1968). Reformed governments, perhaps more apt to stress middle class policies directed toward the entire community, are shown to favor higher levels of expenditures in recreation–culture than nonreformed governments, and do so under more "middle-class" conditions. Nonreformed governments, however, are characterized as favoring particularistic policies more responsive to lower income groups and ethnic factions. The data do not show them operating in this manner; nonreformed systems spend greater amounts for health under the opposite of low-income conditions, and reformed governments are shown to excell in social expenditures more apt to be demanded by lower income groups.

Even within the contrasting political systems the separate political attributes show differential abilities to distinguish between levels of expenditures under varying social and ecological conditions. For example, in the area of safety, form of government is related to expenditure differences under a greater variety of conditions than either type of elections or form of representation. Much the same occurs in other expenditure categories. In general, form of government is shown to be the most important political characteristic for differentiating between levels of expenditure, followed by the index of reform. (An important exception to this is in the area of economic development–housing, where form of representation is most important.) Given these differences in ability to distinguish between expenditure levels, generalizations regarding the spending priorities of reformed and nonreformed governments may be less useful than discerning the particular attributes involved.

The analysis has also shown that a number of social and ecological variables also appear to be important correlates of revenue sharing expenditures, and in certain instances may be more important than political characteristics. This is particularly true of region, and appears most clearly in the safety category, as well as for transportation, environment and health. In each instance both intraregional homogeneity and interregional heterogeneity in expenditures is indicated.

The importance of region as a condition affecting policy decisions has been noted in other contexts (e.g., Wolfinger and Field 1968) and is likely to be due to a number of separate conditions associated with the different regions, including historical development (such as time periods in which major urban growth occurred), regional politics and traditions, differential needs for particular types of funds, and the varying social and economic compositions of cities within these regions. Given this, it is important that the associations between levels of expenditure and political characteristics be analyzed on a regional basis. This latter analysis showed a substantial reduction in the expenditure differentials between the two forms of political system, as well as indicating some reversals from the patterns found at the national level. The strongest of these regional patterns are summarized as follows (read each as containing the phrase "under selected social and ecological conditions").

1. East—reformed systems tend to spend more than nonreformed for social services and development.

2. South—nonreformed systems tend to spend more than reformed for health.
3. Midwest—reformed systems tend to spend more than nonreformed for social services; nonreformed governments tend to spend more for transportation.
4. West—nonreformed systems tend to spend more than reformed for health.

Beyond region, other variables that were shown to be significantly associated with expenditures were metropolitan status and income. For transportation, recreation–culture and social services and development, reformed governments in central cities show higher levels of expenditure than reformed suburban systems. For transportation and health, high-income cities show the lowest level of expenditures.

Conclusions

One rationale of the revenue sharing program is to give local communities the opportunity to expend increased funds in ways determined by local priorities and conditions. Assuming this to occur, we would have expected significant degrees of variation in expenditure patterns according to variations in community political, social, and ecological characteristics, since such characteristics are likely to reflect different political priorities and program needs. Our analysis has shown that such variations occur to only a limited extent. On the average, cities of different political types tend to follow similar expenditure patterns, allocating the largest proportion of their funds to safety and the smallest to social services and education. While differences in the percentages allocated to the nine expenditure categories do vary, they do so by only a few percentage points. Generally, only in the case of safety expenditures do markedly different percentage allocations occur by cities with different political systems.

Within this general framework of similarities, reasonable differentiation in expenditures does occur by political, social, and ecological characteristics, but only when all cities are considered nationally. For cities within each of the four regions much less variation occurs, particularly when communities are differentiated by social and ecological variables in addition to political ones. Intraregionally, significant variations in expenditures occur in only three categories—social, health, and transportation—and only in the latter category is the level of expenditures relatively high. While all of these differences are of academic interest, they are of limited usefulness for policy purposes.

If must be remembered that our analysis concerns funds received at the very outset of the revenue sharing program. As such, allocation decisions may not reflect longer term trends. One may also guess that during this early period allocations were made mostly to those areas that would win general community support. With time and assurances of continued revenue sharing funds, local governments may begin to allocate larger shares of their funds to other areas, and this is likely to produce greater variation in expenditure patterns among cities.

References

Aiken, Michael. 1970. "The Distribution of Community Power: Structural Bases and Social Consequences." In Michael Aiken and Paul E. Mott, eds., *The Structure of Community Power,* pp. 487–525. New York: Random House.

Banfield, Edward C., ed. 1968. *Urban Government.* New York: Free Press.

Caputo, David A., and Richard L. Cole. 1973. "General Revenue Sharing: Initial Decisions." *Urban Data Service Report,* 5 (December 1973). Washington, D.C.: International City Management Association.

Caputo, David A., and Richard L. Cole. 1974. *General Revenue Sharing: The First Actual Use Reports.* Washington, D.C.: Office of Revenue Sharing, Department of the Treasury, March.

Clark, Terry N. 1968. "Community Structure, Decision Making, Budget Expenditures and Urban Renewal in 51 American Communities." *American Sociological Review,* 33(August): 576–93.

Crain, Robert L., Elihu Katz, and Donald E. Rosenthal. 1969. *The Politics of Community Conflict.* New York: Bobbs-Merrill.

Froman, Lewis A. 1967. "An Analysis of Public Policies in Cities." *Journal of Politics,* 29(February): 94–109.

Greenstone, David J., and Paul E. Peterson. 1968. "Reformers, Machines and the War on Poverty." In J.Q. Wilson, ed., *City Politics and Public Policy,* pp. 267–92. New York: John Wiley.

Hawley, Amos. 1963. "Community Power and Urban Renewal Success." *American Journal of Sociology,* 68(January), 422–31.

International City Managers Association. 1967–68. Municipal Yearbook. Chicago: International City Managers Association.

Lineberry, Robert L., and Edumnd P. Fowler. 1967. "Reformism and Public Policies in American Cities." American Political Science Review, 56(September): 701–16.

U.S. Bureau of the Census. 1972. Census of Population, 1970. Washington, D.C.: U.S. Government Printing Office.

Wolfinger, Raymond E., and John Osgood Field. 1968. "Political Ethos and the Structure of City Governments." In Terry N. Clark, ed., *Community Structure and Decision Making,* pp. 159–95. San Francisco: Chandler.

3

Measuring the Effects of General Revenue Sharing: Some Alternative Strategies Applied to 97 Cities

Catherine Lovell

The Measurement Problem

Measuring the effects of general revenue sharing on recipient governments presents some interesting and complex methodological problems. Certain types of effects, which may be thought of as input effects, are relatively simple to measure. These effects result from the primary distributional impacts of the money—how much each recipient government gets, the relation of these amounts to their budgets, comparisons of these amounts with those received from other grant programs, and analyses of what types of recipient jurisdictions gain and lose by the distribution formula. This type of distributional information is readily available allowing straightforward descriptive analyses and correlations to answer the question thought to be relevant at this level. The central problem at this level is the development of the important questions. The data to answer the questions may be obtained entirely from published sources: entitlement amounts, census data, etc., and the researchers need not go near the recipient governments.

The measurement of a second level of effects, the throughput or decision process effects, is slightly more difficult requiring first-hand observation of the processes, or interviews with focal actors about the procedures they used in making allocational decisions about the uses of the new funds. Deciding about the important questions is the main research problem at this level also.

The third and final level of measurement, finding the *real impact* of the new funds on the expenditure and revenue patterns of the recipient

Funds for the larger study on which this chapter is based were provided by the National Science Foundation, Contract #SSH-75-00189. The research was conducted by this author and John Korey and Charlotte Weber. Funds for additional analysis of the data were provided by the University of California. However, any opinions, findings, conclusions, or recommendations expressed herein are those of the author and do not necessarily reflect the views of NSF. Tod Larson assisted with the data analysis and display for this article

49

jurisdictions and identifying the programmatic impacts on the citizens, presents the most difficult as well as the most important measurement challenges. This level of GRS measurement has received the least attention methodologically. It is the most expensive and the approaches that have been tried are the most controversial. Obviously, measurement must precede evaluation and *informed* policy decisions cannot be made until measurement problems are solved and some agreement is found among researchers about the important questions and their answers. Although the fiscal impact questions represent only a part of the body of relevant questions about GRS, they have seemed to be the questions that most concern members of Congress and the general citizenry. Extensive disagreement still remains; the differences result from differences in measurement methods.

In the following pages several alternative strategies used to measure the GRS effects on the governments of 97 southern California cities are described and the methods and findings are compared with those of several other research studies.[a] The findings from the California study at the first two levels are described very briefly; third-level measurement problems and tentative findings are treated in more detail.[b]

Data for the California cities study were gathered from the following sources: (1) annual expenditure and revenue data about all California cities are published by the office of the California State Controller;[1] (2) the list of GRS entitlements to each government jurisdiction published by the U. S. Department of the Treasury;[2] (3) budget and other financial documents of each city; (4) Actual Use Reports filed by each city with the Department of the Treasury;[c] and (5) interviews with city managers, finance officers, and political leaders.[d]

---

[a] The cities, each with a population 10,000 or more (1970), are located in a geographic area formed by two contiguous urbanized areas in Southern California: The Los Angeles–Long Beach area, covering southern Los Angeles and northern Orange Counties; and the San Bernardino–Riverside area, which is immediately east of the Los Angeles–Long Beach area, and consists of portions of southwestern San Bernardino County and northwestern Riverside County.

[b] For a detailed discussion of the research findings, see Catherine Lovell, John Korey, and Charlotte Weber, *The Effects of General Revenue Sharing on Ninety-Seven Cities in Southern California,* Final Report to the National Science Foundation, June 1975. For further development of the fiscal impact methodology, see Catherine Lovell and John Korey, "Measuring the Fiscal Impact of General Revenue Sharing," paper presented at the 1975 Annual Meetings of the American Political Science Association, San Francisco, California, September 2–5, 1975.

[c] Each recipient government is required to file an Actual Use Report form listing the various allocations of GRS funds to each of the listed functional categories. Copies of these reports were obtained from each city.

[d] A structured interview instrument was prepared. Interviews were conducted by the study authors with the help of two graduate students, Kris Jensen and Derick Brinkerhof. Copies of the instrument are available on request.

Primary Distributional Impacts—The First Level

During the first three years of revenue sharing, the 97 California cities averaged $7.85 per capita GRS receipts annually. For the average city, these receipts constituted 5.1 percent of all revenue and 6.4 percent of nonearmarked revenue (those revenues the cities are free to allocate as they wish, without earmarking by the state or federal government or as a part of tax law). Such funds constituted a major portion of the "new money" available to the cities FY's 1972–73 and 1973–74. In FY 1972–73, the first full year in which the cities received GRS funds, they constituted a median of 38 percent of the increment to total revenue and 40 percent of the increment to nonearmarked revenue. In only 14 percent of the cities was GRS a fifth or less of the increment to total revenue and in only 5 percent did it fail to exceed a fifth of the nonearmarked revenue increments for these California cities. These findings agree with other research findings. According to extensive nationwide studies of the impacts of the GRS distribution formula, GRS may be as much as 33 percent of the total budget of some small, limited-function governments, or as little as 2 percent of the total budget of some large governments; however, the nationwide average is 5 to 6 percent.[e]

The GRS formula was designed to benefit recipient governments with low-income populations as well as to reward governments with high tax effort (that is, those governments making most use of their own revenue sources). In studying our California cities we found that *city population wealth* and *city government resources* present two quite different dimensions, thus providing a convenient basis for separate analysis of these two components of the distribution formula.

Annual GRS receipts per capita ranged from a low of $4.14 in two cities with both high *population wealth* and high *city government affluence* to a high of $30.10 per capita for two cities (both industrial enclaves) with a very low *population wealth* and extremely high *city government* affluence. Through a simple correlation test between GRS and selected measures of the affluence of city populations and of city governments, a fuller description of the redistributive effects of GRS among this group of California cities was gleaned. We found moderate tendencies for cities with populations having low-income profiles to receive more GRS funds per capita than cities with affluent populations; also, in general, GRS

---

[e] For confirmation of these figures see Richard Nathan et al, *Monitoring Revenue Sharing,* Washington, D. C.: The Brookings Institution, 1975, and *General Revenue Sharing, Research Utilization Project,* volume 1, Summaries of Formula Research, Superintendent of Documents, U.S. Government Printing Office, Washington, D. C, 1975 (hereafter cited as *NSF GRS Summaries*).

funds have constituted a relatively large percentage of the budgets of cities with low-income populations.

A somewhat different picture emerged, however, when we looked at the affluence of the city governments rather than the affluence of their inhabitants. City governments rich in other sources of revenue tended to receive more GRS funds than resource-poor cities, although the former are somewhat less dependent on such revenue than the latter. The most likely explanation for this is found in the California procedure for distributing sales tax revenues to cities at point of sale rather than on a population or some other more redistributive basis. This has resulted in some cities receiving enormous revenues from this source, and thus appearing to have high tax effort, when, in fact, many are not heavily exploiting their own resources in the "true" tax effort sense.

In short, while the per capita income portion of the distribution formula appears to have produced a redistributive effect, the tax effort portion of the formula seems to have backfired for this particular group of cities. A perusal of findings from the nationwide research on this subject shows variation in comparative distributional effects along these dimensions depending on the tax laws in particular states.[3]

An important question about GRS is how its distributional effects are "different" from those of categorical grants. In all but 16 of the cities GRS per capita was larger than the per capita amount received from categorical grants. Thirty-three of the 97 cities had never received a federal grant before GRS except for the emergency employment funds in the years just prior to GRS.

By correlating GRS and categorical grant receipts (each measured both in per capita terms and as a percent of total revenue) with selected sociodemographic characteristics of city populations, we found that GRS is somewhat more redistributive than categorical grants in terms of absolute levels of funding and a good deal more redistributive in terms of city government's dependence on such funding.

We found also that the distribution of the two forms of federal aid to cities with high concentrations of black residents have been quite different from the distribution to cities with proportionally large Spanish-heritage populations. The high-percent-black cities have clearly benefitted more from categorical grants than from GRS, while the reverse has been true for cities with proportionally large Spanish-heritage populations.

We also correlated GRS and categorical grants with various measures related to city government affluence and found, as mentioned above, that cities already rich in other resources such as sales tax receipts generally receive more GRS funds per capita than cities poor in other resources. By contrast, there appears to be little relationship between city government affluence and categorical grant receipts.

From our interviews and observations it seems clear to us that different kinds of city behavior are rewarded under the two systems. Whether a city is a high-categorical-grant city seems to depend on perceived role, predisposition toward federal aid, and ability at grantsmanship (a combination of initiative, expertise, energy and salesmanship); under GRS the formula determines the distribution.

We know of no other studies as yet that have compared the distributional impacts of GRS and categorical grants among cities so we cannot compare our data with other researchers' findings along these dimensions.

Decision Process Effects—The Second Level

Measurement at this level is not a problem primarily of quantitative analysis but rather focuses on the selection of relevant questions. Answers may be obtained through questionnaires, interviews, or observation. The Brookings Institution national study, and the various National Science Foundation funded studies have generally agreed on the important questions in this area, focusing on the political and structural impacts. All the studies, including our California study, found only minimal structural impacts on such political processes as governmental consolidations, annexations, or special district formation rates.[4] All the studies found that GRS did not have a substantial impact on budget or planning processes.[5] The studies generally agreed, also, that GRS resulted in very little increased citizen input to budget processes.[6] All agree, also, that the antidiscrimination portions of the GRS act have had little effect on the discrimination practices of recipient governments.[7]

The importance of these findings from a methodological standpoint is the extent to which there is general agreement about them regardless of the measurement method used. The findings were similar whether obtained by mailed questionnaires as in the Caputo–Cole study, or by telephone interviews as done by Opinion Research Corporation and the Stanford Research Institute, or by the structured interviews as in the Michigan Institute for Social Research national survey and in our California study, or by informed observer analysis as conducted by the Brookings Institution study and our California study.[f] Although there has been some small argument about the validity of certain sampling techniques used in the various studies there has been relatively little disagreement among the researchers about either the general methodological approaches or the findings at this level of measurement.

---

[f] For a complete description of the various research studies, see the *NSF GRS Summaries*, volume 5.

The Fiscal Impacts—The Third Level

Measuring the fiscal impacts of GRS presents the most difficult and interesting challenge.[g] Unless we can understand with some certainty what the recipient governments do with the GRS money we have no grounds for evaluating programmatic impacts nor for attempting to relate sociodemographic variables (such as size, income levels, race, etc.) or political system variables (such as governmental form, voting behavior, etc.) to various GRS policy outputs. In other words, understanding the real nature of the decisions—how GRS has affected expenditure levels for various programs, and/or has affected the jurisdiction's own revenue sources—is a prestep to all other analysis at this level.

The Fungibility Question

The question about the uses to which GRS money is being put by recipient governments is far from the straightforward one it may seem to be at first glance. In order to ascertain the real fiscal effects of the program, researchers have had to deal with what has come to be known as the fungibility problem.[h] The GRS allocations come to the recipient governments with only minimal strings attached and although priority expenditure categories are included in the federal legislation, they are so broad that they have little impact on the use of funds. To the recipient government, the money is simply a revenue increment that is gratefully received and allocated through local resource allocation methods. The recipient government need only record and report to the U. S. Treasury Office of Revenue Sharing the objects or activities to which it *first* allocates the money, and be sure to assign the money within 24 months of date of receipt.

The process of finding out how the local governments have assigned the money is simple and straightforward if one is interested *only* in the first allocation of the shared funds and not in the final resting place of money that might be displaced by such fund assignment. In this context, then, fungibility means that money from one source can substitute for or displace money from another source. In other words, the significant question of how the spending and revenue patterns of the recipient

---

[g] Some observers have taken the position from one point of view that how the recipient governments spend the money is irrelevant since they see decentralization of program decisions as an end in inself and the principle purpose of the GRS program. For them, it is sufficient to know that recipient jurisdictions are, in fact, making their own decisions with a minimum of federal interference.

[h] For an additional discussion of the fungibility question, see the *Brookings Study,* pp. 182–84.

governments are affected by the new money can be answered only if the final resting place of displaced money can be found.

General revenue sharing, just as any other increment to revenue, can affect expenditure and revenue patterns as well as the cash position of the city. When GRS is introduced into a city's revenue picture it can either be *additive* to general funds or *substitutive* for funds that would have otherwise been raised from other revenue sources. When GRS is actually allocated to a functional area it can either add to the funds that would normally have been spent on that function if GRS were not in the picture, or it can substitute for other funds that would have been allocated to that function. If GRS is substitutive for funds that would have otherwise been allocated to a particular function the funds that GRS displaced can either be moved to another function or distributed across many other functions or put in reserve funds, or not raised at all.

In short, answers to two questions must be found:

1. Was GRS:
   a. Additive to expenditures in one or more functional areas? If so, which area(s) and how much was added?
   b. Additive to total revenues? If so, how much was added?
   c. Additive to reserve funds? If so how much was added?
2. Was GRS substitutive for other revenues? If so for which source(s) of revenues and by how much?

Estimating the final resting place of the money, essential to an understanding of the actual fiscal impact of GRS at the recipient level, is therefore extraordinarily difficult.

Alternative Measurement Methods

The data for measuring fiscal impact have been, for the most part, obtained by researchers in five different ways: (1) from the Actual Use Reports, (2) from questionnaires mailed to recipient government officials, (3) from interviews with recipient government officials, (4) from the judgments of experienced observers, (5) from trend analyses of changing patterns of revenues and expenditures before and after the introduction of the GRS money. (This latter method has been used in only two studies that we know of to date, ours and the study conducted by Tom Anton.)[8]

Our California cities project collected data on each of the 97 cities by methods 1, 3, 4, and 5. Comparisons of the data collected by each method convinced us that most of the data on fiscal impact collected in the first four ways is likely incorrect and in some cases absurd. Each of the sets of data present quite different findings.

In the following sections I describe the findings obtained from methods 1, 3, and 5, show how they compare to another, and present an evaluation of the accuracy of each. The data collected by method 4 is not compared here because those data were unavoidably influenced in the course of collection by the trend analysis we were conducting (method 5) at the same time.

Actual Use Reports and Interview Data on Expenditures by Functional Categories Compared with Actual Budgetary Dollar Increments.

Table 3-1, which follows, displays and compares the data on mean percentages of expenditures of GRS funds by functions in the 97 cities as reported in interviews and as listed on the Actual Use Reports Analysis of variance was conducted to test for interaction *between* the 2 groups of data and *among* the 18 common expenditure categories. The results indicated

Table 3-1

Mean Percentages of Expenditures of GRS Funds by Function Comparisons between Actual Use Report and Interview Data, All 97 Cities Combined, Fiscal Year 1973–74

	Actual Use Reports FY 1973–74	Interview Data FY 1973–74
Operations and Maintenance		
Public safety (fire and police)	25.8	19.8
Environ. protection	1.9	0.4
Public Transportation	1.7	0.9
Health	0.2	0.9
Recreation	1.1	1.1
Libraries	0.2	0.1
Soc. serv., aged & poor	0.4	0.6
Financial administration	0.5	0.3
Capital Expenditures		
Multipurpose & gen. govt.	10.9	12.1
Education	0.0	0.0
Transportation	4.0	3.2
Social Development	0.7	0.4
Housing & comm. development	1.7	1.4
Economic development	1.0	1.0
Environmental conservation	3.4	3.2
Public safety	13.4	11.4
Recreation/Culture	19.1	27.9
Other	4.2	9.8

Note: Analysis of variance testing for interaction *between* the 2 groups of data and *among* the 18 common expenditure categories indicated there was a significant difference at the 0.05 level of significance.

that there was a significant difference between the Actual Use Reports
and the Interview Data at the 0.05 level of significance.

As we see by table 3-1, although there is a statistically significant
difference between allocations to the various expenditure categories as
reported on the Actual Use Reports and in the interviews, the real
differences are not great. While this might suggest that the two
approaches confirm one another, a more probable explanation is that each
produces generally similar results because each suffers from similar
shortcomings.

In order to get a "real life" idea of the accuracy of these data we
compared these findings to actual budgetary data. Since the interview and
Actual Use Report data are so similar only the former was used in the
analysis now described. A sample of ten cities was selected for the
comparisons. The methodology used in selecting the ten cities is rather
complex, and a detailed discussion of it would be well beyond the scope of
this chapter. Briefly, a combination of factor analysis and hierarchical
cluster analysis was used to develop a grouping of cities such that each
group would contain cities with similar socioeconomic, political, and fiscal
profiles.[i] The procedure resulted in a ten-fold clustering of cities. From
each cluster, that city nearest the cluster centroid (i.e., having a profile
most similar to that of the cluster as a whole) was selected for more
detailed analysis. The ten cities thus selected, referred to as centroid cities,
were used as a sample.

Table 3-2 serves as an example of the analysis conducted. It shows:
(1) the dollar amount by which each major expenditure category increased over the previous year, (2) the dollar amount of GRS that the city
officials said they had allocated to the category, (3) the percent that the
GRS allocation reported in the interviews was of the dollar increment, (4)
the percent that the increment was over that of the previous year, and (5)
the average increment that the city has spent in that category over the six
years prior to GRS. A comparison of the columns should give the reader a
good indication as to whether the GRS funds allocated were substitutive
for other revenues in the category or additive to the normal increment.
All figures have been deflated to *constant* dollars to control for inflation.
Since the last two years, in particular, have been such high inflation years
normal increments in *actual* dollars would be misleading.

In the centroid city for Cluster 1, displayed in table 3-2, we see that
the interview data indicates assignment of $49,358 of GRS funds to fire
and $417,078 to public works. First, looking at the fire category, we see
that the amount of $49,358 allocated to fire by the interview data would be

---

[i] For a detailed discussion of the clustering methodology see chapter III of Lovell, Korey,
and Weber, *Effects of General Revenue Sharing,* June 1975.

Table 3–2
Comparison between Dollar Increments Spent in Functional Categories and Interview Data, FY 1973 and FY 1974 (Centroid City of Cluster 1: Middle Class Suburban)
(In Constant Dollars)

	A	B	C	D	E
	$ Amount City Spent in Category Over Previous Year's Expenditures	*$ Amount of GRS Reported by Interviews as Spent in Category*	*GRS Allocation as Percent of Increment (Equals Column B/ Column A)*	*$ Amount City Spent in Category Over Previous Year (Column A) Computed as Percent*	*Average Increment in Category for the Six Years Prior to GRS*
General government	211,544	0	0%	18%	15%
Police	–9,804	0	0%	–1%	6%
Fire	8,555	49,358	573%	1%	3%
Public works	892,357	417,078	46.7%	99%	10%
Parks and recreation	30,677	0	0%	13%	60%
Health	0	0	0%	0%	0%
Libraries	0	0	0%	0%	–33%
Other	–71,913	0	0%	–36%	–11%

573 percent of the year's increment for the expenditures. Also, fire expenditures were up only 1 percent over the previous year, while the "normal" increment (the average of the previous six years) was 3 percent. In this case it should be fairly clear that any GRS allocated to fire would be substitutive for other funds, thus freeing them up to move somewhere else.

In the case of public works, the interview data indicated assignment of $417,078 to that category which would make up 46.7 percent or nearly one-half of the amount of the increment. The increment, however, was 99 percent over the previous year's while the "normal" before GRS increment was only 10 percent. In this case the GRS funds were very clearly additive.

Looking at the increment in spending in the parks and recreation category we see an increment of 60 percent over the previous year. Although the officials did not say, or perhaps even realize it, some of the freed up money from fire conceivably funged into this area.

Similar examination of tables on the other nine sample cities revealed similar findings. They confirmed the doubts we had developed about the interview data and, by association, the Actual Use Report data, as well as demonstrating the complexity of the displacement problem.

We turn next to the third set of methods by which the fiscal impacts were measured.

Regression Analyses

As another way of getting at the real fiscal impact of GRS we conducted bivariate and multivariate regression analyses of trends in the cities' expenditures by function (police, fire, public works, etc.) revenues by source. Based on our belief in the interrelationships between expenditure levels and revenue generation potentials and on our belief in the incremental nature of budgeting, we hypothesized that significant variations from "normal" trends in spending and in city-controlled revenues coincident with the introduction of GRS would be good indications of the fiscal impacts of GRS.[j]

Data for a nine-year period were collected for each city: however, data from the first four years of the nine were not included in the various

---

[j] Most studies of budgeting have stressed its incremental nature. Among the most influential studies of municipal budgeting with which our views are consistent is John P. Crecine, *Governmental Problem Solving: A Computer Simulation of Municipal Budgeting* (Chicago, Rand McNally, 1969), "A Simulation of Municipal Budgeting: The Impact of the Problem Environment," in W. D. Coplin, *Simulation in the Study of Politics* (Chicago, Markham Publishing Company, 1968) pp. 115–46.

analyses because we were concerned that conducting the analysis over too long a period, and including data from a period with a vastly different political and economic context would obscure fiscal patterns prevalent at the time GRS was introduced.

Space here does not permit detailed discussion of the three regression techniques as applied.[k] In summary, the bivariate analysis was conducted between GRS (coded as a dummy variable, that is, "one" for the two years following the advent of GRS (FY 1972–73 and 1973–74) and "zero" for the three years preceding the introduction) and various categories of receipts and expenditures. These categories are measured in terms of increments (or decrements) to the previous years' figure. Increments are computed on a per-capita basis in order to control for differences in city size. All figures were converted to constant dollars before increments were computed.[l] This was done in order to control for the effects of inflation, which were more severe in the later years of the period studies.

Computing changes in budgetary patterns in terms of increments provides a useful focus because (1) GRS funds make up a relatively small percentage of cities' revenues (5.1% average during the first three years of the program), but a large percentage of the increments to revenues (average 38%), and (2) there is a considerable body of literature that concludes it is with respect to such increments, and not to total receipts, that budgetary decisions are made.[m]

In the trivariate regression analysis the GRS dummy variable was replaced by two dummy variables, one representing FY 1972–73, the other FY 1973–74, in order to determine more precisely when the effects described below occured.

In the multivariate regression analysis the dependent variables were defined as above, and independent variables were (1) dummy variables for FY 1972–73 and FY 1973–74, (2) the increment to the category of the dependent variable for the prior year (in the expectation that the increment in one year would provide a good predictor of the increment in

---

[k] See Lovell, Korey, and Weber, *Effects of General Revenue Sharing,* June 1975, for a full discussion of the premises. For details on applications of the three regressions see Lovell and Korey, "Measuring the Fiscal Impact of General Revenue Sharing."

[l] In controlling for inflation the Implicit Price Deflator for State and Local Government (see Council of Economic Advisers, *Economic Report of the President,* January 1975) was used to adjust both expenditures and revenues. Although this is not the most accurate deflator for local governments in California, tending to underestimate inflation, it is the best deflator readily available. (For an excellent discussion of the most common deflators and the drawbacks associated with them see David Greytak, Richard Gustley, and Robert J. Dinkelmeyer, "The Effects of Inflation on Local Government Expenditures," *National Tax Journal,* volume 27, December 1974, pp. 583–98.

[m] See Crecine, *Governmental Problem Solving,* and "A Simulation of Municipal Budgeting" for discussions on this subject.

the next), (3) the category of the dependent variable as a proportion of total receipts (excluding GRS) or expenditures in the prior year (in the expectation that the larger the category as a percent of the budget, the larger would be its increment). For the categories "property tax increment," "other local revenue increment," and "current service charges increment," the "constant dollar per-capita increment to sales tax" was also included as an independent variable, based on the hypothesis that a large per-capita increment to the sales tax would enhance the possibility of reductions (or at least postponement of increases) in other revenue sources.[n]

The results from all three of the regressions indicated that, associated with the advent of GRS, there were significant declines in the increments in constant dollars (the purchasing power) to those sources of revenue subject to control by the cities (property taxes, miscellaneous local revenues, and current service charges), but not in sales taxes whose rates are beyond the control of the cities, at least in the short run, and are taxes that are positively affected by inflation. This finding suggests that a major impact of GRS has been to substitute for increments to own-source revenues and for losses due to inflation.

On the expenditure side of the ledger, the regression data suggested there was a major increase, associated with the GRS program, in capital expenditures, distributed across various functional areas. The analysis provided *no support at all* for the contention (suggested by all the research studies based only on Actual Use Reports or on questionnaire and interview data) that the public safety functions have been primary beneficiaries of the GRS program. On the contrary, in all three of the regressions, GRS seemed to be associated with *declines* in the increments to police and fire expenditures. While it would be absurd to suggest that addition of GRS funds to city budgets had anything to do with such declines, the data at the same time completely fail to support the

---

[n] The formula used was:

$$Y_i = a + b_i \, \text{LAG} + b_i \, \text{PCT} + b_i \, \text{SALES} + b_i \, \text{FY 1973} + b_i \, \text{FY 1974} + e_i$$

a = a constant.
LAG = the constant dollar per-capita increment to the category i in year $t-1$.
PCT = the receipts and expenditures in category i in year $t-1$ as a percent of the total receipts (excluding GRS) and expenditures in year $t-1$. This variable was not used in the equation for tax rate.
SALES = the constant dollar per-capital increment to sales tax in year t (only used in certain equations—see text).
b_i = the regression coefficients.
e_i = random error.
FY 1973 and FY 1974 are dummy variables. For discussion of the use of dummy variables, see Daniel B. Suits, "Use of Dummy Variables In Regression Equations," *Journal of the American Statistical Association,* LII, December 1957, pp. 548–51.

hypotheses that GRS has produced additional increments in these categories.

The regression conclusions are presented with great caution, since there are alternative explanations that are at least as consistent with the findings. Measuring increments in constant dollars may distort a decision-making process in which actors think in terms of actual rather than constant dollars. Another difficulty is that, at about the same time that GRS was introduced, other changes were taking place in the cities' environments, particularly inflation and recession. It would be virtually impossible, using the regression approach, to separate the effects of these other changes from those of GRS. It should be noted that the presence or absence of GRS explained only a small fraction of the total variance in budgetary increments. Even the most complicated model, the multivariate, succeeded in explaining only, at most about a third of total variance—in most cases, the figure for explained variance was lower. Until we know what factors account for most of the residual variance, findings from the regression analysis must be regarded as tentative.

Property Tax Rates and Expenditure Trends

In an attempt to verify the effect of GRS on own-source revenues found in the regression analyses the property tax rates of each city were examined for changes. These changes were examined in relation to the overall revenue picture—that is, changes in revenue from each other source. Property-tax rate changes provide, perhaps, the best direct measure of the policy decisions made by the cities in response to fiscal needs. Although California cities depend heavily on the sales tax (about a third of their revenues) the state basically sets the rates; therefore the largest source of revenue over which the cities have almost exclusive rate control is property taxes.

The examination showed that property tax rates have, on the average, increased each year, yet assessed valuation and therefore revenues derived from this source have decreased in terms of real purchasing power.

Total revenues increased by less than 2 percent in FY 1973–74 over FY 1972–73; sales taxes increased by about 4 ½ percent and revenue from other agencies, which includes GRS, increased by about 10 percent. At the same time property tax revenues decreased by approximately 10 percent. Revenues from service charges decreased very slightly also.

Although the examination did not provide absolute evidence that GRS was substitutive for additional increments to property tax rates, it does seem plausible that if the cities were to maintain existing levels of service *in the absence of revenue sharing* It would have been necessary to increase other sources of revenue. No sources for change other than property tax were readily available to the cities.

Trend graphs by annual percentage increments were constructed for each of the principle city expenditure categories. Although space does not permit display of those graphs, we found that corrected for inflation and population, expenditures for public works, fire, and police did not increase at all or increased by much lower amounts in FY 1973–74 than over the former year. Parks and recreation showed an absolute decrement over the previous year's allocations. General government was the only expenditure category showing a larger increase in FY 1973–74 than in the previous year.

Again, these data on incremental changes are not definitive proof of the effects of GRS. They did, however further confirm our doubts about the validity of Actual Use Report, questionnaire, and interview data (our own included), which showed the principle fiscal impact of GRS as being on expenditures in the safety areas of police and fire.

A final note on the expenditure side strengthens even further our concern in this area. The recently released (November 1975) *Governmental Finances in 1973–74* makes it possible to include that year in a trend picture of nationwide expenditures by local governments. A brief glance at police spending by local governments is presented in table 3–3.

Table 3–3
Annual Increments to Police Spending by Local Governments in the United States, FY's 1969–70 through 1973–74, Actual Dollars

Fiscal Year	Local Police Expenditures in Billions—Actual	Percent Annual Increase
1969–70	3.81	
1970–71	4.43	16.3
1971–72	5.08	14.5
1972–73	5.69	12.1
1973–74	6.14	7.9

Source: Compiled from *Governmental Finances, Fiscal Years 1969–70, through 1973–74*, U. S. Department of Commerce, Bureau of the Census.

Table 3–3 shows the five years decline in percent increases in police spending with a dramatic decline in FY 1973–74, which was the first year encompassing significant expenditures of GRS. Carefully constructed time-series studies including FY 1974–75 will be necessary before further real clues to the final impact of GRS on local governments nationwide can be found.

Conclusion About Fiscal Impact Measurement

An examination of the various data and comparisons among them convince us that it is in a sense far easier to demonstrate how *not* to measure the fiscal effects of the GRS program than to show how (or even whether) such measurement can be accomplished. As this, and every other major research project has shown, Actual Use Reports clearly do not provide reliable estimates of the fiscal impact of GRS funds.[9]

To a slightly lesser degree, doubt is also cast on the validity of questionnaires and interviews as an approach to the fiscal effects measurement problem. This is especially true when interview questions are framed in a manner similar to the format used in the Actual Use Reports, that is, officials are asked about what they "spend the money on" rather than about the net fiscal effects (on both revenues and expenditures). The problem is not that local officials deliberately falsify answers but that the officials themselves do not really know the answers. In one of the NSF-funded, mailed questionnaire studies of state officials, for example, a great deal is disparity was found among the answers from officials of the same state about what they believed to be the fiscal effects in their state.[o] In essence, officials were being asked the purely hypothetical question of "what would have happened if GRS funds had not been available?" Even the most sincere and informed answer to this kind of question is, at best, educated guesswork heavily affected by the environment of uncertainty in which the budgetary process takes place.

In our California cities research, as I have demonstrated, there was significant disparity between what the interviews indicated about fiscal impact and what careful examination of trends revealed. Our final conclusion is that further longitudinal analysis and applications of econometric techniques will be necessary before anything can be said with absolute validity about fiscal impact. It is our belief that there was probably more impact on the revenue trends of recipient governments than on expenditure patterns.

Overall Conclusions

Based on our experience in attempting to measure the effects of GRS on one large group of recipient jurisdictions it is my conclusion that a great deal of interesting and relevant data has been accumulated at two levels of measurement. The information desired at these levels lend themselves to

[o] See discussion of state research conducted by Deil Wright, *NSF GRS Summaries*, volume 4.

questionnaire and interview techniques. Measurement at a third level, the fiscal impact, however, has not been solved and is perhaps insuluble with any degree of validity at this stage in the history of the GRS program. Therefore, any analyses or interpretations about GRS that depend on fiscal effects analysis should be regarded as questionable. Valid data is simply not available to assess program impacts on various types of citizens or to compare variations in allocation decisions among different types of jurisdictions.

At this stage, evaluation of the GRS program by researchers, members of Congress, or the general citizenry cannot be based on hard fiscal effects data but must be based on intuitive impressions derived from a careful examination of the various pieces of research combined with a healthy degree of caution, or on the findings at the first two levels of measurement.

Notes

1. *Financial Transactions Concerning Cities in California,* Annual Reports, Controller, State of California, Sacramento, California.

2. *Data Elements, General Revenue Sharing Entitlements,* United States Department of the Treasury, Superintendent of Documents, Washington, D.C.

3. *General Revenue Sharing, Research Utilization Project,* volume 1, Summaries of Formula Research, Superintendent of Documents, U. S. Government Printing Office, Washington, D. C., 1975 (hereafter cited as *NSF GRS Summaries*).

4. *NSF GRS Summaries,* volume 4, and *Brookings Report.*

5. *NSF GRS Summaries,* volume 4, and *Brookings Report.*

6. *NSF GRS Summaries,* volume 4, and *Brookings Report.*

7. *NSF GRS Summaries,* volume 4.

8. Thomas J. Anton, University of Michigan, *Understanding the Fiscal Impact of G.R.S.,* Final Report to National Science Foundation, June 1975.

9. *NSF GRS Summaries,* volumes 2 and 4.

4

The Political Ingenuity of the Revenue Sharing Act

Kent Eklund and Oliver P. Williams

The United States Congress, long famed for its skill in forging complex political compromises, may have achieved another milestone in its own tradition of artfulness in the Revenue Sharing Act. The layers on layers of compromises embedded in the final formula led congressmen themselves to ask, after its passage, "What hath we wrought?" This mystery about revenue sharing has proved a bonanza for social science research. The largely federally financed outpouring of evaluation research can be divided into two kinds.

The first asks if the results of the actual distribution of funds is in keeping with the apparent intentions of Congress. While the congressional debate included discussion of redistributive measures designed to aid hard pressed property tax payers, in the final formula, this objective was layered over by other considerations. Still, it is reasonable and relevant to ask what the redistributive effects of the act are and whether "hard pressed" local governments do stand to gain more than others. Now that the act is operational do we find clear beneficiaries whose needs would never have moved Congress to act in the first place?

The second type of research asks what behavioral changes are induced by revenue sharing. Since the act was supposedly intended to aid local governments to do what they were otherwise unable to do, the primary changes have to do with local policies. The requirement for reporting uses of funds clearly indicates congressional concern and interest in this area. One can also raise questions about another range of behavioral changes. What kinds of ingenuity are being employed by individual governments to increase their take under the formula? The act clearly provides incentives for reliance on taxes, rather than user changes, in financing local services. General-purpose governments are given advantages over special-purpose ones, and some "do-nothing," general-purpose governments are also rewarded.

This chapter exemplifies the first type of research, involving a search

---

The data used for this study was gathered through the support of NSF, Grant #36028.

for unintended or unpredicted beneficiaries of the act. Any act as complex as this one is bound to have some distributive effects that become manifest only after the transfer payments are actually made. In the case of the Revenue Sharing Act, this might result from the setting of maximum–minimum limits, apportionment among jurisdictions, and unforseen correlates of the official weights, income, and general tax effort.

There are many factors that affect the fiscal well-being of local governments, in addition to those that were built into the revenue sharing formula itself. For example, some populations are more expensive to service than others, and the same is the case for certain kinds of land use. While the Revenue Sharing Act focuses on general-purpose local governments, municipal finance is also fiscally affected by the pattern and cost of services performed by special districts, not the least of which are school districts; all of these are excluded from benefits under the terms of the act. Finally, age or the stage of development may have fiscal affects; for example, old cities may have a worn out physical infrastructure in need of replacement. Thus, we explore three sets of fiscal factors (1) the municipal profile, (2) the school district environment, and (3) community age. None of these, it must be stressed, were specifically recognized in the revenue sharing formula.

Locus of Study

The results of this inquiry are more germane to municipalities in metropolitan areas, particularly to those that are governmentally fragmented. Because our national population largely dwells in metropolitan areas, and because in these areas fragmentation is increasing more rapidly than consolidation, the concern of the chapter is relevant to much of the country. The reason for making the distinction between metropolitan and nonmetropolitan settings is that urbanization creates areal specialization. All urban systems are characterized by variety and complexity, which is reflected in territorial organization. The political units, that is, the suburbs, satellites and cities in a metropolitan complex, are all areal fragments of a larger social and economic system. Furthermore, each municipality in a metropolitan area is unique; indeed, the very resistance to metropolitan consolidation is based upon their desire to protect and preserve "uniqueness." While the units are literally unique, they can also be arrayed along various continua. Here, we look at the interaction among some of these variations in municipal specializations and revenue sharing.

Although our analysis is confined to the urbanized portion of the Philadelphia SMSA, in some respects our findings have more general applicability. Because of the apportionment scheme of the act, every county has a unique fiscal environment under revenue sharing. However, viewed in another perspective, the municipalities in all metropolitan areas are affected similarly because of the characteristic differences among them. There are older and newer areas, richer and poorer, residential and industrial, etc.

The urbanized portion of the Philadelphia SMSA is an area that embraces 202 municipalities in 8 counties in 2 states. The area is defined as the contiguous band of townships, boroughs, and cities around the core city, which have at least 300 persons per square mile. This definition excludes nearly an equal number of municipalities around the outer fringe of the SMSA. These rural or small town units do not display the forms or degree of specialization characteristic of the urbanized inner lying municipalities.

The Philadelphia area has its variety of newer municipal suburban units distributed across the middle-class spectrum (including two Levittowns), older, in-lying residential suburbs beginning to filter down, old industrial satellite cities (Chester and Camden) and smaller versions of some (e.g., Conshohocken), as well as a sprinkling of more exotically specialized municipalities. Most metropolitan areas have approximate counterparts; hence, that which follows could probably be written about any one of them, although smaller metropolitan areas usually have lesser extremes of specialization.

The Municipal Profiles: "Fiscal Winners and Fiscal Losers"

Every student of local government knows that the politics of each unit in metropolitan areas has an overlay of considerations designed to attract the "right" kind of people and exclude the "wrong" kind. School, land use, and even sewer policy often involves these kinds of concerns. "Right" and "wrong" is an euphemism for a combination of race and status and fiscal concerns. In developing the municipal profile we are primarily concerned with the latter, hence, the term "fiscal winners and losers." Extrapolating from some of the Charles M. Tiebout and Albert O. Hirschman[a] arguments, we pose the question: What if suburbs could pick their own population and economic base? Creating a mythical local city council that wants to minimize municipal problems, we ask what would

_____

[a] There are scores of studies that were inspired by Charles M. Tiebout, "A Pure Theory of Local Expenditures," *Journal of Political Economy* LXIV (October 1956), pp. 416–24; and Albert O. Hirschman, *Exit, Voice and Loyalty* (Cambridge, Mass.: Harvard University Press, 1972).

be its likely choices. We assume that the mythical council would want citizens who caused few problems and who could pay more in taxes than they cost in services. Following this line of reasoning, we have constructed a municipal profile of winning and losing indicators. They are as follows:

Age

Mature adults are not only in their prime productive years from an income standpoint, but are also the most active population with respect to community and civic support. They are the age group least likely to need public care and require costly facilities. Unlike the fixed income elderly, they are more likely to be able to pay taxes. On the other hand, the most costly age group is school age children. Thus, our mythical community ought to maximize the adult (not retired) percentage of its population and minimize the number of its children. The "winner" and "loser" age indicators chosen were percentage population 45 to 64 years old and percentage 5 to 14.

Education

A professional, college-educated population is likely to provide more in civic support, maintain consistent employment, and generate fewer needs for welfare services than an elementary educated one, thus, the two indicators: percentage of population with four or more years of college and percentage with only elementary education.

Occupation

The same line of reasoning used for education led to the choice of proportion of employed citizens in high status occupational (professional and managerial) and low status (operatives, transport workers, and laborers) categories.

Income

Obviously, high-income families have a greater ability to pay for their service needs than do low income ones. The indicator was the percentage of households in each municipality in the $25,000 and above and in the

$2,000 to $6,999 categories. The first category represents approximately the top five percent of families, the second about 25 percent. Experience has shown that the below $2,000 category has many peculiar characteristics, probably with great overrepresentation of the very young and old. The selection was designed to highlight the categories most prized and most despised by the fiscal chosers.

Family Size

The lexicon of every local councilman includes reference to the costly large family with many children, as opposed to the profitable childless couple. Thus, we posited small families as "winners" and large families as "losers" for our indicators.

Industrial Specialization

Of all broad types of land use, industry is generally judged to have the best cost–revenue ratio for municipalities; thus, we have used percentage of total value industrial use as a "winner" and percentage residential as a "loser."

Residential Value

It is not possible to have a municipality without some residents, so all else being equal, it is better to have large, expensive private homes than inexpensive small ones. Thus, the top and bottom metropolitan quintiles for value per household were used as indicators. The source is the census declaration by home owners as to the value of their house.

Apartments

The matter of apartment houses is controversial among local government officials. There is no clear consensus about whether or not to have them. Sentiments are often against apartment building in the suburbs, but this may be more symbolic than fiscal: Apartments are, after all, the symbol of center city; still, recent court cases may put an end to suburbs without them. Again, if there must be apartments, it is better to have luxury ones than those which attract "problem populations." The former are usually very large and contain many units. The "worst" are the converted house and the small apartment. Two pairs of indicators were chosen to deal with the apartment situation: High rents and one-unit structures were coded desirable; low rents and structures containing two to four households, undesirable.

Housing Condition

Most of the traditional housing condition indicators of the census have so little variation they are useless. Plumbing and central heating, for example, are nearly universal. However, we coded old housing (built before 1939) as an indicator of impending deterioration and excessive crowding (more than 1.01 persons per room) as a further sign of abuse or overuse of housing stock. No comparable winning indicators were paired with them.

Revenue Sharing

Finally, to complete the analysis, annual revenue sharing receipts per capita was computed, based on the first four entitlements, as well as a ratio of revenue sharing to total municipal expenditures.[b]

The frequent use of extreme values, rather than the overall distribution of populations in many of the foregoing indicators, is justified by more than the views of our hypothetical councilman. As yet unpublished findings by the authors on the same metropolitan area indicate that between 1950 and 1970 there is a tendency for municipal specialization to increase in terms of many of these winner and loser categories. That is, while the bulk of the middle range of values on most status and other demographic and housing characteristics tend to be distributed over the enlarged metropolitan area of 1970 in a fashion similar to the distribution of 1950, this is not also true for the extremes. The tails of the distribution tables tend to attenuate, indicating increased municipal specialization among the highs and lows.

Given the use of 20 indicator variables, in addition to revenue sharing per capita and the revenue sharing–municipal expenditure ratio, a factor analysis was employed in a preliminary way to deal with problems of intercorrelation. The objectives were to test whether there was, indeed, a winner and a loser factor, and whether or not the revenue sharing indicators loaded on the losers. As table 4-1 indicates, there is not one winner–loser factor but, in fact, four, and revenue sharing per capita has a

---

[b] The first four entitlements divided by 1.5, divided by 1970 total municipal expenditures.

relationship with only one Principal, varimax, and oblique pattern and structure matrices were computed with the results of the latter being reported. Oblique rotation was chosen, as the analysis does not require the identification of orthagonal factors. Employing parental prerogative in naming the factors, we refer to them in order as (1) primary status, (2) family, (3) industrial specialization, and (4) secondary status.

Table 4-1
Municipal Indicators: Factor Structure, Oblique Rotation

	Factor			
Variable	1	2	3	4
Pct. college educated (W)	0.905			
Pct. high income (W)	.939			
Pct. professional occupation (W)	.900			0.584
Pct. high house value (W)	.871			
Pct. high rental (W)	.674			
Pct. elementary educated (L)	−.711			−.732
Pct. low income (L)	−.529			−.772
Pct. low status occupation (L)	−.717		−0.569	−.592
Pct. low house value (L)				−.790
Pct. low rentals (L)			−.500	−.658
Age, pct. 45 to 64 (W)		−0.674		
Age, pct. 5 to 14 (L)		.894		
Pct. small families (W)		−.824		
Pct. large families (L)		.821		
Pct. 1 family units (W)		.779		
Pct. 2-4 family units (L)		−.648		−.496
Pct. old housing stock (L)				−.781
Pct. crowded units (L)	−0.694			−0.492
Pct. land use industrial (W)			−.858	
Pct. land use residential (L)			.840	
Revenue sharing per capita			−0.674	
Revenue sharing ratio		0.482		

		Eigenvalue	Pct. of Variance
W—winners	Factor 1	7.755	35.2
L—losers	Factor 2	4.614	21.0
	Factor 3	2.016	9.2
	Factor 4	1.439	6.5
			71.9

Among the findings of interest are that winning and losing indicators invariably have opposite signs if they load on the same factor. Fortunately, all winning and losing attributes are not related, so there is some distribution of both good and bad fortune across various municipal units. In spite of the presence of the income weight in the revenue sharing formula, the revenue dollars do not necessarily come in the largest amounts to the municipalities with the largest low status population, nor do they totally elude the grasp of those with the largest higher status. Revenue sharing also seems unrelated to family structure differences, although the revenue sharing–municipal expenditure ratio does load on the family-size factor. This could, of course, reflect comparatively low municipal expenditures as well as modest revenue sharing receipts. It could be that burdensome school costs depress municipal tax efforts, a possibility we explore later.

First, let us turn to the question of whether revenue sharing is as neglectful of low status municipalities as the factor matrix seems to imply. Again, we are purposely not using the weights built into the formula in the analysis. But, by using a somewhat more stringent set of tests, we can ask whether low status municipalities benefit in a redistributive sense. Using an analysis of variance it is possible to illuminate the relationship a little better. Six classes were constructed for two of the status variables, percentages of high income families and low rental units, the latter being the highest loading variable on the secondary status factor.

In Table 4–2 the relationships between revenue sharing per capita and high income is displayed. We find that the difference in means across the six classes is indeed progressive in the predicted fashion; they do cluster in a statistically meaningful fashion. However, the erratic pattern among municipalities in classes #1 and #2, those with small percentages of high-income families, is inconsistent with a linear relationship between revenue sharing and percentage of all families who are in the higher income brackets. Evidently, there are some municipalities with extremely small percentages of the well-to-do who fare both poorly and extremely well on revenue sharing, even when the general relationship between the two variables is along predicted lines.

Table 4–2
High Income and Revenue Sharing Analysis of Variance

Group	Interval	Size	Mean	Variance	Std. Dev.
1	0.0– 2.5%	61	13.24	19.51	4.41
2	2.5– 5.0%	60	9.81	9.30	3.04
3	5.0–10.0%	43	8.99	2.46	1.57
4	10.0–15.0%	12	7.90	0.15	0.39
5	15.0–20.0%	12	7.63	0.29	0.54
6	20.0+	12	6.49	0.19	0.44

Grand total mean = 10.24

Source of Variation	Sum of Squares	Degrees of Freedom	Mean Square
Between	944.11	5	188.82
Within	6,354.10	194	32.75
Total	7,298.22	199	

$F = 5.77$ $(P < 0.01)$

With regard to percentage low rentals (table 4–3), again the differences in classes are consistently along redistributive lines. Although, over one-half the municipalities are lumped together in class #1 because they have negligible (under 2%) low-rent housing, the pattern evens out rather smoothly for the remaining municipalities, which have an appreciable amount of the low-rent housing stock. While the analysis of variance reveals significant class differences, there is obvious overlap among classes in terms of revenue sharing receipts.

Table 4–3
Low House Value and Revenue Sharing Analysis of Variance

Group	Interval	Size	Mean	Variance	Std. Dev.
1	0– 2%	107	8.12	5.57	2.36
2	2– 5%	38	10.56	6.58	2.56
3	5– 7%	13	11.47	2.30	1.51
4	7–10%	12	12.72	1.87	1.36
5	10–20%	21	15.20	6.94	2.63
6	20+	8	18.70	4.96	2.22

Grand total mean = 10.24

Source of Variation	Sum of Squares	Degrees of Freedom	Mean Square
Between	1,676.51	5	335.30
Within	5,621.71	194	28.97
Total	7,298.22	199	

$F = 11.57 \ (P < 0.01)$

As it is obvious that the redistributive effects of revenue sharing are present but overlayed and obscured by other factors, a third approach is helpful in revealing the basic pattern. Table 4–4 shows the distribution of revenue sharing measured both by per capita and as a ratio of municipal expenditure in relationship to the percentage of low-income families in a municipality. In each box, the upper percentage pertains to the rows and the lower one to the columns. While many of the rows and columns do scale in a redistributive fashion, there are many significant exceptions. Generally, the revenue sharing per-capita values are more in the predicted direction than those in the revenue ratio ones. (Note the empty cell in the lower right corner of the ratio half of the table.) For an example of an anomolous pattern, observe the 15 to 20 percent row. In per-capita revenue sharing among these 26 municipalities, more units get under $6 than over $20, a reversal of the redistribution direction repeated in the adjacent categories.

Thus far, the analysis of our municipal profile has established that winners and losers are, indeed, birds of a feather that flock together, though there are several species of each. In spite of the failure of the

Table 4-4
Percentage Low Income Families and Municipal Revenue Sharing Receipts, Cross-tabulation

	Per-capita Revenue Sharing								Revenue Sharing Ratio					
	0–$6.00	$6.00–7.99	$8.00–9.99	$10.00–12.99	$13.00–19.99	$20.00+	N	%	0–0.14	15–0.19	0.20–0.24	0.25–0.34	0.35–0.49	0.50+
0–5%	50.0% / 14.0	25.0% / 6.8	8.3% / 2.6	16.7% / 5.1	0% / 0	0% / 0	12	6.0	16.7 / 4.1	16.7 / 5.1	16.7 / 5.1	25.0 / 6.7	25.0 / 16.7	0 / 0
5–7%	20.0 / 16.3	17.1 / 13.6	34.3 / 31.6	17.1 / 15.4	8.6 / 14.3	2.9 / 6.7	35	17.6	28.6 / 20.4	20.0 / 17.9	14.3 / 12.8	25.7 / 20.0	8.6 / 16.7	2.9 / 12.5
7–10%	26.5 / 30.2	22.4 / 25.0	24.5 / 31.6	20.4 / 25.6	4.1 / 9.5	2.0 / 6.7	49	24.6	20.4 / 20.4	18.4 / 23.1	14.3 / 17.9	20.4 / 22.2	2.3 / 5.6	7.0 / 37.5
10–13%	18.2 / 18.6	31.8 / 31.8	18.2 / 21.1	18.2 / 20.5	11.4 / 23.8	2.3 / 6.7	44	21.6	32.6 / 28.6	20.9 / 23.1	16.3 / 17.9	20.9 / 20.0	2.3 / 5.6	7.0 / 37.5
13–15%	18.2 / 9.3	9.1 / 4.5	9.1 / 5.3	36.4 / 20.5	13.6 / 14.3	13.6 / 20.0	22	11.1	18.2 / 8.2	22.7 / 12.8	36.4 / 20.5	18.2 / 8.9	4.5 / 5.6	0 / 0
15–20%	15.4 / 9.3	26.9 / 15.9	7.7 / 5.3	15.4 / 10.3	23.1 / 28.6	11.5 / 20.0	26	13.1	30.8 / 16.3	11.5 / 7.7	30.8 / 20.5	19.2 / 11.1	3.8 / 5.6	3.8 / 12.5
20%–0	10.0 / 2.3	0 / 0	0 / 0	10.0 / 2.6	20.0 / 9.5	60.0 / 40.0	10	5.0	0 / 0	40.0 / 10.3	20.0 / 5.1	40.0 / 8.9	0 / 0	0 / 0
N = / % =	43 / 21.5	44 / 22.0	38 / 19.0	39 / 19.5	21 / 10.5	15 / 7.5			49 / 24.6	39 / 19.6	39 / 19.6	43 / 22.6	18 / 9.6	8 / 4.0

Key: Row %
Col. %

revenue sharing variables to load on the status factors, there seems to be a general redistributive pattern present, but there are obviously other factors operative. To further stretch our metaphor, there seem to be birds that are getting the revenue worm regardless of their status. We can find a hint of the identity of one such species by probing factor three, industrial specialization. In Table 4–5 analysis of variance computations are displayed for revenue sharing per capita and percentage of assessed valuation in industrial usage. The six classes cluster the municipalities in a significant fashion and the difference in means of each group move in a direction to reward the "winners" rather than the "losers." The reason for this apparently stems from the tax effort weight in the basic formula. In municipalities with high proportions of industrial land use, tax increases can be viewed with relative indifference, in comparison with municipalities similar in all other respects but with a smaller industrial tax base. The brunt of taxation is allayed by the industrial cushion. The greater the cushion, the less pressure the tax rate places on residential property. Thus, all else being equal, the industrial municipalities can more easily compile a better tax effort record.

Who are the beneficiaries of this industrial specialization effect? In order to explore this question, the 202 urbanized municipalities of the Philadelphia SMSA were divided into five classes, according to the percentage of total assessed valuation in the industrial category, with the following results:

Under 10%:   143 municipalities
10 to 15%:   16 municipalities

Table 4–5
Percent of Assessed Value in Industrial Property and Revenue Sharing,
Analysis of Variance

Group	Interval	Size	Mean	Variance	Std. Dev.
1	0– 1%	44	7.25	0.98	0.99
2	1– 3%	37	9.33	3.16	1.77
3	3– 8%	23	10.81	2.44	1.56
4	8–17%	37	10.37	9.46	3.07
5	17–48%	29	13.43	9.81	3.13
6	48+	8	19.47	2.69	1.64

Grand total mean = 10.24

Source of Variation	Sum of Squares	Degrees of Freedom	Mean Square
Between	110,597	5	221,193
Within	112,056	194	5,776.10
Total	14,596.4	199	

F = 38.29 (P < 0.01)

15 to 20%:	12 municipalities
20 to 40%:	19 municipalities
40% and over:	12 municipalities

For the 143 municipalities with under 10 percent industrialization, very little of the municipal tax burden is transferred from residential to industrial property owners. However, as we move up the scale in some of the most industrialized units, over half the tax bill is carried by industrial property owners. Cross tabulations were computed for each of the five classes of industrialization, with a number of combinations of other variables.

What are the 12 municipalities in the over 40 percent category like otherwise? In the first place, 10 of the 12 do have above average revenue shares per capita. Only one of these is also above the mean in terms of percentage of wealthy homes, and most are older, industrial areas, characterized by rather large, space consuming factories (several steel mills, refineries, large manufacturing plants), combined with small populations. The one higher status municipality also has a large industrial park. As we move down to the next class of 19 municipalities, with 20 to 40 percent industrial land use, this latter phenomena becomes commonplace. The comfortable suburb with an industrial park, the traditional local councilman's dream, is also a blessing for getting the most out of the revenue sharing dividend as well. This is even clearer when we look at low income in relationship to revenue sharing per capita by industrialization class. There are 141 municipalities with less than 10 percent of property in industry, and of these, 64 were above the mean in terms of percentage low-income families. Of these 64, only 22 had above the mean in revenue sharing receipts per capita. Of the 31 municipalities with over 20 percent of property in industry, 20 were above the mean in poor families and of these, 15 were above the mean in revenue sharing per capita.

The winning attribute in a municipal profile that is not in the formula seems to be industry.

Public Education

The general Revenue Sharing Act is specifically designed for municipalities; educational costs are very self-consciously excluded from any consideration. It may seem unfair, then, to bring up the matter of educational burdens in an assessment of revenue sharing results. The fact remains, however, that municipalities do differ in terms of educational needs, just as it is true for municipal needs. While many states, including

Pennsylvania, and to a much lesser extent New Jersey, use state aid to help the harder pressed school districts, public education nevertheless is a large burden on local taxpayers. To the local taxpayers, the relationship of revenue sharing to school costs is not without interest.

A second set of indicator variables were chosen to reflect some of the relationships between school and municipal finance and revenue sharing (table 4–6). While there was a direct measure of municipal expenditures per capita available; there was no direct way to obtain a comparable school figure, as school district boundaries frequently do not coincide with municipal ones. A school tax rate was derived from local tax records, made possible estimates of effort in relation to property wealth. From census data we know the percentage of population in each municipality in public schools. (Note, in the correlation matrix there is only a 0.65 correlation between this indicator and the percentage of population in the 5 to 14 years of age group.) Market value per capita and percent industrialized are also included as wealth or resource measures and two of the education measures introduced above were included again.

The resulting correlation matrix is a rather lean harvest of significant relationships. The revenue sharing measures are unrelated to either measure of school fiscal circumstance. There is the slightest of associations between percentage of population in public school and the revenue sharing ratio (0.23). But this really tells us very little. The municipalities with the highest revenue sharing ratios are often not those with largest revenue sharing per capita receipts. However, the negative correlations between municipal expenditures (-0.24 and -0.19) and the school need indicators give some indication that the heaviest school burden does not coincide with a municipal one. Further exploration is in order here.

A plotting out of the revenue sharing per capita and percentage of population in public schools variable reveals a nearly U shaped curve; municipalities with the most and the fewest public school children receive the lowest revenue sharing per capita. However, these low and high groups of municipalities on the public school children indicator have no other detectable shared characteristics. Stated differently, the communities that have large school burdens and also receive scant revenue sharing aid include places that are both rich and poor, in both the property and, to a certain extent, the income sense. On the other hand, most municipalities with low school children populations are also low on the revenue sharing receipts. Those in the seemingly most favored spot, fewest children, and most revenue sharing per capita, are, in fact, the old declining industrial areas, including the core city Philadelphia. Paradoxically, while their school population is low, their school budgets are not, so they are hardly candidates for a "windfall" category.

Table 4-6
Correlation Matrix, Municipal and School Fiscal Indicators

	1	2	3	4	5	6	7	8	9	10
1. Revenue sharing per capita	1.00								0.44	0.50
2. Revenue sharing ratio	0.47	1.00							0.06	−0.40
3. School tax rate	−0.05	0.13	1.00						−0.10	−0.24
4. Pct. pop. in public schools	0.05	0.23	0.01	1.00					−0.18	−0.19
5. Pct. pop. 5 to 14	0.01	0.32	0.04	0.65	1.00				−0.22	−0.31
6. Market value per capita	0.15	−0.13	−0.11	0.05	−0.08	1.00			−0.23	0.36
7. Pct. industrial	0.39	0.12	−0.04	0.02	0.01	0.46	1.00		0.26	0.23
8. Pct. college educated	−0.13	−0.17	0.02	0.07	0.12	0.37	−0.20	1.00	−0.78	−0.13
9. Pct. elementary educated	0.44	0.06	−0.10	−0.18	−0.22	−0.23	0.26	−0.78	1.00	0.33
10. Municipal exp. per capita	0.50	−0.40	−0.24	−0.19	−0.31	0.36	0.23	−0.13	0.33	1.00

Rate of Growth

One of our more fixed images of metropolitan structure is that of the differential conditions in the older and newer portions. The frequently noted description includes a core city suffering population loss, property value declines, an accumulation of what we have called "losing" attributes, while the newer suburbs are growing, with a new environment, modern municipal infrastructure, and a population profile likely to support municipal services. As revenue sharing was in part designed to help the hard-pressed cities, it is important to consider the actual flow of revenue sharing aid. Do the old declining parts of the metropolitan areas fare better than the newer ones?

It is difficult to answer the question because metropolitan municipalities always display a great variety of attributes and defy easy classification. A potential indicator of municipal age is the percentage of the housing stock built before 1939, a variable used on the profile analysis. Percent of old housing stock, which loaded only on factor four, has no relationship to the revenue sharing variables. In the correlation matrix, housing age was unrelated to percentage high income, but had a 0.6 correlation with percentage low-income families and the apartment conversion indicator (percent two to four unit apartment houses). A few scatterplots reveal there are newer suburbs with substantial proportions of low-income families and there are a few rich older suburbs. A correlation matrix that included a number of growth indicators based on either population and property value along with the revenue sharing variable again results in 0.0 correlations.

In order to obtain a more direct classification of units, two subsamples of the metropolitan area were drawn; the first includes those units that have had actual population decline since 1950 (N = 28) and the second those fringe suburbs that crossed the urban threshold of 300 persons per square mile between 1960 and 1970 (N = 24). We shall call these respectively the *decliners* and the *new suburbs*. At first glance at a few variables (table 4-7), the pattern is about as we expect.

The decliners have more poor families, more industry, and receive more revenue sharing than the new suburbs, with the balance of the units in the metropolitan area falling somewhere in between. It is with regard to the revenue sharing ratio that the results are somewhat surprising. This is a short-lived mystery, however, when one inspects the municipal budgets of the new suburbs. Here is one of the results of the minimum benefits stipulation in the formula. These new suburbs are among the lowest in municipal expenditures per capita. They simply provide very few services. Even though they lose out on the income and the effort weights in the formula, the minimum means that they obtain a higher percentage of their municipal expenditure dollar from the federal government than do the so-called, hard-pressed, inner cities and older suburbs, which have very substantial municipal budgets. However, they obviously receive much less on a per-capita basis.

Table 4–7
Difference of Mean between Decliners and New Suburbs, Selected Variables

		Percentage Low Income	Percentage Industrial	Revenue Sharing Capita	Revenue Sharing Ratio
Decliners	Mean	15.9	15.9	15.5	0.245
N = 28	S.D.	5.1	22.1	10.8	0.163
New suburbs	Mean	7.5	5.0	8.0	0.298
N = 28	S.D.	3.5	9.5	2.6	0.100
Balance	Mean	10.0	9.1	9.6	0.231
N = 136	S.D.	3.7	13.5	5.6	0.140

One further question needs to be raised about the decliners and the new suburbs. While the differences between them seem clear enough, what about the internal variations within each subsample with respect to revenue sharing? Note in table 4–7 the very high standard deviations for industrialization. As it turns out, only three of the new suburbs have any appreciable industry. (In these cases, percentage industry and revenue sharing per capita are positively related.) The decliners present a somewhat more complex picture that is set forth in table 4–8. Again, the skewed distribution seems to be attributable to the intervening effects of industry. In the bottom two rows, the difference between those in the left and right cells is again industry. Thus, industry not only brings windfalls to municipalities not so much in need, but, with equanimity, brings additional revenue to the not so well off, too.

Throughout this study we avoided using the variables that are part of the revenue sharing formula calculation, but have used other measures of need or condition. However, in a final effort to get some perspective on the industrial effect, we computed a regression equation to predict revenue sharing per capita from percent industrial, percentage of families in the low-income category and municipal expenditures per capita. The latter two are actually surrogates for weights in the formula. The municipal expenditure variable dropped out and the results were:

	Multiple R	R^2	B	F
Low Income	0.5149	0.2651	0.9891	8.128
Pct. Industrial	0.5979	0.3575	0.3856	3.596
Constant = 2.63043				

Table 4–8

Cross-tabulation for Decliners, Revenue Sharing Per Capita by Percentage of Low Income Families

	0–$6.00	$6.00–7.99	$8.00–9.99	$10.00–12.99	$13.00–19.99	$20+	T
0–5%	1	0	0	0	0	0	1
5–7%	0	1	0	0	0	1	2
7–10%	0	0	0	0	0	0	0
10–13%	1	3	0	0	0	0	3
13–15%	1	0	0	1	0	1	3
15–20%	2	3	1	2	3	2	13
20%+	0	0	0	0	1	5	6
T	5	7	1	3	4	9	N = 28

Percent Families Low Income

In summary, while income levels obviously have an effect on the distribution of revenue sharing, as we would naturally expect, industrial specialization maintains an independent influence and probably masks the tax effort weight in this case. In a similar regression equation for the entire metropolitan area, the same two variables are significant in explaining variations in revenue sharing per capita, but the amount of variance explained is only 25 percent.

Two measures of revenue sharing benefits have been used throughout this analysis. We might ask as a postscript who are the doubly favored and the doubly left out, that is, what kind of municipality is low with respect to both revenue per capita and the ratio and vice versa. Operationally, what are the attributes of municipalities in the extreme diagonal cells in a cross tabulation of the two variables?

Those low on both revenue sharing variable tend to be the older, middle-class suburbs, of small to medium size (about 5,000 to 20,000). These suburbs are old and dense enough to have established substantial urban services, but not of the magnitude of the larger satellite cities or the core city. They are without industry, but are not low on the income scale. Indeed, they are the very model of the "nice," mature residential suburb.

The opposite set of cells are thinly populated, with the very extreme one occupied by two relatively low-income, low-density suburbs that provide very little in the way of services but have a little nonresidential tax base. The most industrial municipalities all rank high in revenue sharing per capita but distribute themselves along the mid-range of the revenue sharing ratio scale.

Conclusions and Summary

The Revenue Sharing Act is designed to be an aid to municipalities generally and those with low-income citizens and those that try harder especially. Indirectly, the home owner and property taxpayer are the unnamed beneficiaries, according to design. This study takes an alternative set of assumptions about need and tests them against the initial results of actual revenue distributions. Need is recoded into community attributes that tend to indicate a burden or a relative asset for the municipality. We have often used the extremes of the total population, but in each case they are consequential ones in a policy sense.

If need, defined in these terms, were congruent with the redistributive effects of the Revenue Sharing Act, this should be verifiable by statistical tests. But, use of simple correlations and factor analysis failed to show that the need or cost-generating characteristics were associated with larger revenue sharing receipts, nor did they reveal the opposite. Indeed, it was difficult to find any consistent association with any of the 30 odd variables and revenue sharing. Funds seem to be distributed nearly evenly or randomly among the winners and losers. Analysis of variance revealed that there is, in fact, some correspondence between status factors and revenue sharing but there is substantial variance at each status level.

Effective political action generally depends upon the coalescence of individuals or groups with shared interests. While some are more and some less benefitted by the revenue sharing formula, it is hard to identify the basis for new shared-interest groups arising who are likely to press for substantial revision of the act. This is so in spite of the existence of anomalous cases where negative redistributions seem to occur. Because of the cross-cutting cleavages, few municipalities lose on all counts, but there does appear to be a windfall group. The specialized industrial municipality, often the winner in the property tax lottery of local government, has won once more. While Congress may find itself faced with some who object to the favored few winning again, it is unlikely that other than marginal adjustments in the formula will receive widespread support.

5

Program Evaluation and the Policy Process: The Case of General Revenue Sharing

Edie N. Goldenberg, James W. Fossett, and Thomas J. Anton

Evaluation of policies initiated by governments is generally acknowledged to be both a need and a problem. Each year thousands of laws are passed and tens-of-thousands of directives are issued with no systematic effort to monitor their consequences. Without reliable information about results, continuation or termination of public programs becomes more a matter of conviction than of evidence. Yet, it is far from clear that we know very much about how to do program evaluation. Scholars have developed a variety of investigative techniques, but using such techniques in ways that can affect the policy process is a complicated task. Precisely because we have done so little of it, we have much to learn about effective program evaluation.

General revenue sharing presents an unusual opportunity to advance our understanding, in part because the program was in fact evaluated, in part because there was so much variety in the evaluation techniques employed. In this chapter we review the more salient conclusions generated by the most prominent of several efforts to evaluate revenue sharing, and we attempt to apply those conclusions to important issues in the debate over revenue sharing renewal. We then offer a critical assessment of the extent to which evaluation research results address the issues currently under debate. Since we were participants in major evaluation studies, any criticism should be understood, in part, as self-criticism.

The Results of Research

The State and Local Fiscal Assistance Act poses a number of unusually difficult problems for evaluation. First, it is not at all clear which criteria ought to be used for evaluation. A wide variety of objectives were asserted for the program, by liberals and conservatives, and many of the stated goals were in conflict. All evaluation studies have had to choose, more or

85

less arbitrarily, the value dimensions along which to structure an evaluation, but the criteria applied are not always the same. Second, over 38,000 separate jurisdictions are involved in the program. They vary tremendously in size, function, and capacity. In order to draw conclusions about how the program works generally, it is necessary to examine a number of different types of units. Third, recipient jurisdictions are relatively unrestricted in their use of revenue sharing funds, and "fungibility" makes it difficult to assess GRS impacts. For example, a community may earmark revenue sharing money for a particular use, say public safety, but spend no more on public safety than it would have without revenue sharing funds. In this case, the impact of GRS is not on public safety, but rather on those programs that would have been smaller (or those taxes that would have been higher) in the absence of GRS.

At least three different approaches have been used to try to assess program impact. One relies on survey questions that ask officials how their budgets would have been different in the absence of revenue sharing.[1] Another relies on time-series budget data from a limited number of localities. Estimates of spending in the absence of GRS are derived from the time series and compared with actual patterns of expenditure.[a] The third relies on participant observation, coupled with analysis of fiscal data, to generate judgments about impact—again in a limited number of sites.[2] Each approach was used in at least one of the nine major studies funded by the National Science Foundation in its effort to generate useful evaluation information for the policy-making community.[b] Our review of the major studies suggests that three basic conclusions can be stated regarding the uses to which GRS funds were put.

Use

First, table 5–1 shows that revenue sharing money has not been spent in the same fashion as other local revenues. Before GRS, the ratio of

---

[a] This approach was used in a number of studies. See particularly Thomas Anton et al., *Understanding the Fiscal Impact of General Revenue Sharing* (Ann Arbor: Institute for Public Policy Studies, 1975); Catherine Lovell et al., *The Effects of General Revenue Sharing on Ninety-seven Cities in Southern California* (Riverside: Drylands Research Institute, 1975); and Robin Barlow, "Analysis of Historical Budget Data," in F. Thomas Juster, ed., *The Political Impact of Revenue Sharing,* (Washington: U.S. Government Printing Office, forthcoming), chapter 5.

[b] NSF also funded nine studies that focused on formula change issues, but we do not address those studies here. For a review of the formula studies, see volume 1 ("Summaries of Formula Research") and volume 3 ("Synthesis of Formula Research") of *General Revenue Sharing: Research Utilization Project,* National Science Foundation, Research Applied to National Needs (Washington: Government Printing Office, 1975). The "process" studies referred to here are briefly summarized in volume 2 ("Summary of Process Research") and volume 4 ("Synthesis of Process Research") of the same report.

Table 5–1

Estimates of Fiscal Impact of General Revenue Sharing on Local Governments

Study	Operating Expenses	Capital Expenses	Tax–Debt Reduction– Avoidance*	Other
Office of Revenue Sharing:				
Actual Use Reports[a]				
FY '73	51.1%	48.9%	(44.7%)	
FY '74	52.0%	48.0%	(66.0%)	
Michigan—ISR[b]				
FY '74				
Municipalities				
Over 300,000	68.5%	13.1%	11.1%	7.3%
100,000–299,999	28.4%	27.0%	42.1%	2.4%
Less than 100,000	12.5%	54.8%	17.8%	15.0%
Counties	21.9%	49.0%	13.9%	15.3%
FY '75				
Municipalities				
Over 300,000	51.9%	13.4%	34.1%	.5%
100,000–299,999	30.3%	33.7%	37.6%	−.4%
Less than 100,000	18.9%	50.9%	22.1%	8.1%
Counties	21.9%	42.7%	21.5%	14.0%
Brookings[c]				
FY '73—incl. New York City	17.6%	26.5%	54.8%	1.1%
FY '73—excl. New York City	29.3%	44.3%	24.6%	0.0%
General Accounting Office[d]				
FY '73—250 local gov'ts	67.0%	33.0%	(75.0%)	
FY '74—26 local gov'ts	82.8%	17.2%	(60.0%)	
UC Riverside[e]				
Including Los Angeles				
FY '73	33.9%	28.0%	29.6%	6.0%
FY '74	32.6%	32.3%	20.7%	13.9%
FY '75	46.6%	19.9%	24.5%	8.8%
Excluding Los Angeles				
FY '73	16.3%	59.6%	11.7%	12.1%
FY '74	25.3%	51.1%	16.9%	6.5%
FY '75	34.3%	43.6%	19.2%	2.8%

[a] Sources: For FY '73, D. A. Caputo and R. L. Cole, *General Revenue Sharing—The First Actual Use Reports* (Washington: Office of Revenue Sharing, 1974), 10–13. For FY '74, Office of Revenue Sharing, *General Revenue Sharing: Reported Uses 1973–1974* (Washington: Office of Revenue Sharing, 1975), 37.

[b] Source: F. Thomas Juster, "Fiscal Impact on Local Governments," in *The Economic and Political Impact of General Revenue Sharing,* F. Thomas Juster, ed. (Washington: U. S. Government Printing Office, forthcoming), 31.

[c] Source: Richard Nathan et al., *Monitoring Revenue Sharing* (Washington: Brookings Institution, 1975), 199; and Juster, "Fiscal Impact on Local Governments," 60.

[d] Sources: Comptroller General of the United States, *General Revenue Sharing: Its Use by, and Impact on, Local Governments* (Washington: 1974), 20; and idem, *Case Studies of Revenue Sharing in 26 Local Governments* (Washington, 1975), 8.

[e] Source: Catherine Lovell et al., *The Effects of General Revenue Sharing on Ninety-seven Cities in Southern California* (Riverside: Drylands Research Institute, 1975), 47–48. Lovell and her co-researchers developed, in the course of their research, serious doubts about the validity

operating to capital expenditures for all local governments was approximately 5:1.[3] In spending revenue sharing dollars, the only cities studied that approached this ratio are the largest cities in the Michigan study and the 26 cities studied by the General Accounting Office. Moderately large cities, studied by Brookings and Michigan, show an operating to capital ratio of about 1:1. The ratio for smaller cities is close to 1:4, reversing the normal spending pattern. County governments of all sizes also show an emphasis on capital outlays. The distribution of GRS funds across program areas also differs from that of other revenues. In particular, public safety and amenities appear as major winners of revenue sharing money.[4]

Second, differences between how GRS and other funds are spent are declining over time. As table 5-1 shows, while the uses of GRS are still more capital intensive than usual, noncapital uses increased over the first three years of the program. One major reason for this change is that increasing numbers of local officials appear to be thinking about and allocating funds in roughly the same way they handle other money.[c] The initial GRS checks were received and allocated in many localities under conditions that encouraged their being treated as "special." The receipt of checks out of phase with the normal budget cycles of many localities, the considerable publicity surrounding the program, and the concomitant reduction of a number of federal social programs all appear to have increased the "visibility" of many initial decisions about how revenue sharing funds were spent. Evidence suggests that this increased visibility affected the way revenue sharing funds were spent.[5]

Third, available research is almost unanimous in finding that prior financial conditions are important to explaining variations in how revenue sharing was spent. Local governments in reasonably good financial condition prior to receiving GRS were more likely to use the funds to expand services or to construct new facilities. Hard-pressed governments, on the other hand, were more likely to use revenue sharing to support ongoing programs or to stabilize or reduce taxes.[6]

A fourth general conclusion, growing out of these studies, is that Office of Revenue Sharing (ORS) reports are unreliable guides to

(Table 5-1 Notes, *continued*)
of interview data on fiscal effects. For cautions about the data displayed here see chapter 3 in this book.

* Figures in Tax-Debt Reduction/Avoidance Column are percentages of local officials indicating GRS had impact on taxes rather than percentage of funds used.

[c] This general trend is noted in several studies. See Lovell, *The Effects of General Revenue Sharing*, pp. 55-56; and Edie Goldenberg, "Citizen Participation in General Revenue Sharing," in Juster, *Impact of Revenue Sharing*, chapter 9.

understanding fiscal or program impacts of GRS.[d] Compared to research estimates, ORS reports overestimate impact on public safety and underestimate the impact on general government expenditures and tax reduction. Accounting convenience and political convenience are the principal explanations offered for these discrepancies.

Strings

Few restrictions were placed on how GRS money could be spent, but the effects of two specific strings have been examined. Evidence (Table 5-2) suggests that the priority categories and the prohibitions against using GRS funds to match other federal grants resulted in more use of revenue sharing funds for public safety, private transportation and amenities, and less use for education, social programs, and environmental protection than would otherwise have occurred.[7] Given the easy fungibility of revenue sharing money, the net effect of the priority categories probably has been rather small. The no-match prohibition, however, appears to have exercised considerably more real influence on the way revenue sharing was spent. While ORS regulations allow the use of revenue sharing to supplement grant programs, they prohibit the use of released funds as match, and they require the maintenance of sufficiently detailed records to insure that the prohibitions were not violated.[8] Compared to alternate uses of funds, use of GRS money in areas covered by other federal grants may therefore have been unduly burdensome from an accounting viewpoint. Many local officials, particularly those disposed to use revenue sharing for other programs, may have overinterpreted the requirements or simply concluded that the extra effort of setting up a separate account and maintaining detailed records was not worth the trouble.

There is also evidence to suggest that the no-match and priority category strings prevented some local governments from addressing vital problems. Officials who reported that the restrictions had an impact on their allocations were less successful in spending GRS funds on their most important local problems than were those who reported no effect. As before, the effect of no-match appears stronger than that of the priority categories.[9]

---

[d] Anton et al., *Understanding the Fiscal Impact,* pp. 116–19; Lovell, *The Effects of General Revenue Sharing,* pp. 49–52; Richard Nathan et al., *Monitoring Revenue Sharing,* (Washington: Brookings Institution, 1974), pp. 183–84. The strongest statement of this argument is made in Comptroller General, *Revenue Sharing: Its Use by, and Impact on, Local Governments* (Washington: Government Printing Office, 1974).

Table 5-2
Estimates of the Program Impact of General Revenue Sharing on Local Governments

Study, Fiscal Year	Public Safety	Environmental Control	Land Use, Planning	Trans-portation	Amenities	Educa-tion	Health	Social Services	Financial, General Government	Other	Total
Office of Revenue Sharing[a]											
Actual Use Reports											
1973	35.4%	10.1%	1.9%	20.1%	7.3%	1.3%	7.5%	2.2%	12.8%	1.4%	100%
1974	36.0	11.0	2.0	19.0	9.0	1.0	7.0	2.0	14.0	0.0	100
Michigan—ISR[b]											
1974											
Municipalities											
Over 300,000	15.1%	13.8%	1.2%	9.6%	19.9%	6.2%	11.6%	0.2%	4.9%	17.5%	100%
100,000–299,999	31.6	8.7	6.2	5.5	18.7	2.2	7.1	2.7	6.3	10.8	100
Less than 100,000	32.9	22.8	1.3	22.7	9.3	0.1	9.9	0.0	0.4	0.6	100
Counties	25.8	4.2	7.3	18.9	6.0	7.8	5.7	2.6	4.7	17.0	100
1975											
Municipalities											
Over 300,000	18.4%	14.8%	1.2%	9.6%	16.0%	6.2%	12.5%	0.1%	3.7%	17.5%	100%
100,000–299,999	44.0	11.1	5.0	4.5	14.2	2.2	2.0	0.8	5.2	10.9	100
Less than 100,000	22.5	22.8	3.1	22.5	12.9	0.2	0.5	4.6	5.3	5.6	100
Counties	26.5	0.8	2.5	20.6	8.1	2.7	9.5	4.5	6.8	18.0	100
Michigan—IPPS[c]											
5 cities, 1973–75	42.2%	11.3%	1.2%	0.0%	2.7%	0.2%	6.2%	0.7%	44.2%	9.3%	100%
UC Riverside[d]											
Including Los Angeles											
1973	55.7%	16.0%	0.0%	5.4%	1.7%	2.1%	0.5%	1.5%	8.2%	8.6%	100%
1974	50.7	6.6	2.1	5.2	19.5	0.0	0.4	1.6	5.4	4.9	100
1975	15.8	15.4	1.8	8.5	16.1	0.0	0.2	.66	9.3	33.3	100
Excluding Los Angeles											
1973	27.5%	2.6%	.14%	5.7%	33.0%	0.0%	1.0%	1.8%	11.1%	16.2%	100%
1974	26.4	4.3	2.8	7.9	32.5	0.0	0.9	3.0	10.6	12.5	100
1975	30.8	4.3	4.1	3.6	19.6	0.0	0.0	3.0	10.3	22.3	100

General Accounting
Office[e]

1973	39.0%	6.0%	0.0%	9.0%	3.0%	0.0%	5.0%	2.0%	1.0%	(34.0%)	100%
1974	57.3	10.6	0.0	4.9	10.1	0.0	9.0	2.6	5.5	0.0	99.4%

[a] Source: D. A. Caputo and R. L. Cole, *General Revenue Sharing—The First Use Reports* (Washington: Office of Revenue Sharing, 1974), 10–13, and Office of Revenue Sharing, *General Revenue Sharing: Reported Uses 1973–1974* (Washington: 1975) 37.

[b] Source: F. Thomas Juster, "Program Impact of Revenue Sharing," in F. Thomas Juster, ed., *The Economic and Political Impact of General Revenue Sharing,* (Washington: U.S. Government Printing Office, forthcoming), 10, 11.

[c] Source: Thomas Anton et al., *Understanding the Fiscal Impact of General Revenue Sharing* (Ann Arbor: Institute of Public Policy Studies, 1975), 115.

[d] Source: Catherine Lovell et al., *The Effects of General Revenue Sharing on Ninety-Seven Cities in Southern California* (Riverside: Drylands Research Institute, 1975), 43–44. For cautions about the data displayed here see chapter 3 in this book.

[e] Source: Comptroller General of the United States, *General Revenue Sharing: Its Use by, and Impact on, Local Governments* (Washington: 1974), 20; idem, "26 Local Governments," 8. FY 1973 data are for operating expenses only; "other" category includes capital.

Process

Beyond the initial entitlement period, GRS has had little impact on local budgetary processes. As suggested above, the first revenue sharing checks were probably seen as "special." Not surprisingly, as table 5–3 shows, many cities and counties apparently held special hearings on these initial GRS funds. A smaller number appointed special citizen advisory committees. By 1974 fewer special hearings were held. Within a fairly short time, some cities and counties that initially looked upon GRS as special money that required special public hearings began to treat it like any other revenue.

Table 5–3
Citizen Participation Mechanisms in Revenue Sharing Allocations

	Initial Hearing Held	1974 Hearing Held	New Advisory Committee Formed	N[a]
Municipality				
Population size				
Over 300,000	64.5%	56.2%	14.2%	9
100,000–299,999	62.5	19.6	9.2	32
25,000–99,999	50.5	27.3	6.4	188
10,000–24,999	53.2	18.7	5.9	82
2,500–9,999	40.1	16.6	2.1	63
Less than 2,500	32.1	10.8	0.8	64
All municipalities	38.6	14.6	2.0	438
County				
Population size				
w/in SMSA—over 500,000	44.1%	34.2%	10.3%	28
w/in SMSA—150,000–500,000	44.6	26.3	9.9	31
w/in SMSA—less than 150,000	45.6	27.2	6.5	25
Outside SMSA	56.4	30.1	4.3	26
All counties	54.8	29.8	4.7	110

Source: Edie Goldenberg, "Citizen Participation in General Revenue Sharing," in *The Political and Economic Impact of General Revenue Sharing,* edited by F. Thomas Juster (Washington: U.S. Government Printing Office, forthcoming) 7, 12.

[a] These N's are approximate and conservative since in some cases there were no responses to a particular question and since the lowest N for the three separate questions is shown.

This decline in citizen input does not reflect any widespread aversion to hearings or citizen committees. Survey evidence suggests that most local jurisdictions hold at least one regular public hearing on the budget each year, and a number have citizen advisory committees.[10] Considering hearings and committees together in table 5–4, one can see that very few larger local governments have neither. Most smaller places have one or the other. The decline in special treatment of revenue sharing funds seems to reflect the absorption of revenue sharing into the regular budgetary process.

Some expected that revenue sharing would increase the capacity of local governments to address locally defined problems. The data, however, do not support this expectation. Respondents in the Michigan survey indicated that revenue sharing had relatively little impact on their budget process beyond providing extra money. It did not make it easier to discover community preferences, to establish priorities, to make tax decisions or to control local expenditures. Moreover, local governments appear only modestly successful in spending revenue sharing on programs that address problems of local significance.[11] Clearly, revenue sharing has not substantially expanded the capacity of local governments to deal with "locally defined" problems.

Table 5-4
Coincidence of Regular Public Hearings and Advisory Committees

		Cities Over 100,000 Population (N = 45) Regular Hearings		Cities Under 100,000 Population (N = 491) Regular Hearings	
		No	Yes	No	Yes
Regular	No	0.9%	26.7%	32.8%	50.2%
Committees	Yes	6.9%	65.5%	1.7%	15.4%

		Counties Over 250,000 Population (N = 49) Regular Hearings		Counties Under 250,000 Population (N = 82) Regular Hearings	
		No	Yes	No	Yes
Regular	No	5.4%	56.0%	18.6%	58.1%
Committees	Yes	3.7%	34.9%	0.3%	23.0%

Another expected impact was attributed to the program's five-year authorization. Early expectations were that the program's impermanence would increase uncertainty in local budgeting that would lead local governments to spend the funds on nonrecurring expenditures rather than on operating programs. Available results are ambiguous on this point. While capital expenditures have consumed a larger share of revenue sharing than they do of general revenues, it is not clear that this can be attributed to the program's uncertainty. On the one hand, the Brookings field observers reported that GRS's five-year limit had an impact on the allocation processes of nearly two-thirds of the jurisdictions surveyed and that this impact was largest in cities with large capital outlays.[12] The Michigan survey data further support, with some qualifications, this view that uncertainty has had some impact on how local governments have spent their funds. Table 5-5 presents bivariate relationships between three different measures of uncertainty and the percentage of revenue sharing funds spent on capital projects in FY 1974. Concern about continuation appears to be generally associated with capital spending.

On the other hand, further evidence suggests that the effects of uncertainty were reinforced and possibly accentuated by city characteristics that allowed officials to view revenue sharing funds as "slack."[e] A large literature on local budget making argues that capital accounts are generally the first categories cut and the last increased in the event of revenue changes.[13] Placement of new revenues in capital accounts, in this view, is an indication of general financial well-being. Cities with high capital spending demonstrated characteristics consistent with this argument. These cities were more likely to be in good financial condition, both in the view of the Brookings observers and in the view of local officials, and to be free of pressing service demands from large poor populations.[14] In these cities, revenue sharing seems to have been seen as a windfall that was invested in accelerating capital expenditures. Capital expenditures motivated by the view of revenue sharing money as slack would not necessarily be affected by the certainty of funding.

Table 5-5
Uncertainty and Capital Outlays

Item	Percentage Indicating "Uncertainty"	Beta	Marginal R^2	N
Uncertainty as a major problem				
Cities over 25,000	7.3%	0.1721[a]	0.0296	282
Cities less than 25,000	7.7	−0.0097	0.0001	296
Counties	9.8	0.0692	0.0048	142
Uncertainty leads to spending on capital				
Cities over 25,000	85.9%	0.2467[a]	0.0608	282
Cities less than 25,000	81.0	0.0455	0.0021	296
Counties	82.6	0.2515[a]	0.0632	142
Programs should be made permanent				
Cities over 25,000	19.2%	0.0883	0.0078	282
Cities less than 25,000	15.7	0.1871[a]	0.0350	296
Counties	20.7	−0.0628	0.0039	142

Note: Betas are from bivariate regression of dummy variable on percentage of revenue sharing spent on capital for FY 1974. The first and third variables were constructed from responses to open-ended questions; the second, from closed-ended question.

[a] t ratio > 2.0.

---

[e] For a fuller description of these results in the context of a completely developed model, see Wilensky, "Modelling the Fiscal Impact of Revenue Sharing," in Juster, *Impact of Revenue Sharing*, pp. 11–12.

Participation

The only requirement relating to citizen participation in the 1972 act was that localities publish Planned and Actual Use Reports in local newspapers. It is now recognized that the published reports were neither effective in generating citizen involvement in GRS decisions nor in conveying accurate information about government intentions and actions. A nationwide survey completed in the fall of 1974 found only 10 percent of the general public "claim to have read or heard about about the planned or actual use of revenue sharing funds in their community."[15] A Stanford Research Institute study of ten large cities found that only 11 percent of the public could provide a basic definition of GRS, and only a small percentage of this informed group had any idea of how revenue sharing funds were spent in their community.[16] Furthermore, we now know that those few people who think they learned from the published reports how GRS funds were spent were probably mistaken.

According to official estimates in the Michigan survey, GRS generated little citizen interest and activity in local budgetary matters. Except in large cities, revenue sharing tended to have no impact at all on the level of public interest in the budget. Only the large-city mayors reported attendance increases at budget hearings or group criticism because of GRS. Group interest in GRS was more commonly reported, but most interested groups were well-established, local organizations rather than new groups formed specifically in response to revenue sharing.[17]

One factor contributing to participation increases was the loss, actual or potential, of categorical grants in some jurisdictions. Nearly 45 percent of large-city mayors and over 35 percent of all county executives indicated that revenue sharing expenditures were affected by the actual or potential loss of other grants. As expected, fewer small-city mayors reported such effects. Moreover, concern over the loss of federal funds was positively related to perceptions of citizen activity and interest in revenue sharing in all types of communities. Critical groups and increases in attendance were reported by twice as many large-city and large-county executives who expressed concern over the loss of other federal money as by those who did not. Substantially more small-city and small-county executives reported group interest if they were concerned over the loss of other federal funds than if not.[18] To the extent that citizen activity over revenue sharing was a reaction to discontinued categorical grants, one might expect participation to increase initially and then to decline over time as groups either succeed in establishing a claim to new money to replace the old or as they cease to be viable organizations because of a lack of funds.

Table 5–6
Mean Percent of Revenue Sharing Expenditures for Health and Social Services by Participation Variables for Cities and Counties

(Estimates for FY 1974 Using Survey Data with Equal Dollar Weights)

	Hearings		Advisory Committee		Attendance Increase		Critical Groups		Interested Groups	
	Yes	*No*	*Yes*	*No*	*Yes*	*No*	*Yes*	*No*	*Yes*	*No*
Municipal executives	1.4%	0.5%	1.1%	0.5%	2.8%	0.8%	4.2%	0.4%	1.0%	0.2%
County executives	9.5	26.9	4.6	19.8	18.5	15.2	7.5	15.5	16.9	12.4

[a] Estimates of program impacts using census weights instead of equal dollar weights yield mean percents very close to those cited above. See Juster, chapter 3, for a more detailed discussion of both weighting schemes.

Source: Edie Goldenberg, "Citizen Participation in General Revenue Sharing," in *The Political and Economic Impact of General Revenue Sharing,* edited by F. Thomas Juster (Washington: U.S. Government Printing Office, forthcoming) 24.

Citizen participation in GRS decisions, while limited and sporadic, is associated with particular expenditure patterns in places where it occurs. Table 5-6 summarizes the results. Cities with revenue sharing hearings, committees, or reported citizen involvement spent more GRS money on health and social services than other cities did.[19] By and large, the reverse is true for counties, although attendance increases and expressions of group interest in counties are associated with higher social service expenditures.

Some further data suggest one possible explanation. Officials in localities with hearings, committees, or some form of participation tend to report they pay attention to new problems as a result of revenue sharing. Furthermore, it appears that the new problems these particular officials pay attention to tend to be social services in cities and things other than social services in counties.[20] It is possible that the types and interests of citizens participating at the city level are substantially different from those participating at the county level, and that these differences have produced different expenditure patterns. It is important to remember, however, that higher levels of social service expenditures are not necessarily a consequence of citizen activity but that both may instead result from other causes.

Structure

A final conclusion of some interest can be reported briefly. Although none of the research revealed any significant impact on the division of responsibility between governments, there is evidence of considerable interest in using GRS to induce structural change. In the Michigan survey, state finance officers and House and Senate Appropriations Committee chairmen in each state legislature were asked whether they thought that GRS had encouraged "the continued existence of inefficient units of local government." Most thought so.[21] The belief that revenue sharing has "propped up" inefficient units is stronger among lower house (60.5%) than upper house (45.9%) chairmen, and is strongest in the North Central (70%) and southern (66.7%) states. Officials traditionally thought of as being closest to their constituencies, in short, are most likely to accept the "prop-up" hypothesis in areas where there are large numbers of townships and rural units to prop up.

Officials in these areas, moreover, seem willing to contemplate rather drastic action: two-thirds of the North Central fiscal officers, 60 percent of lower and 55 percent of upper house appropriations chairmen expressed support for a proposal to change the revenue sharing formula "to omit very small government units." Although their colleagues in other parts of the country were less willing to take such drastic action, it is clear that they, too, are willing to do something: nationwide, some 69 percent of state fiscal officers and 67 percent of appropriations chairmen support the use of revenue sharing to "encourage" small-unit consolidation. Officials from small, local units disagree strongly, but they apparently are no longer in control of state legislatures. Urban and suburban representatives now command state governments, and they seem quite willing to push for structural change.[22]

One might sum up the research results with several key terms: initial "specialness" followed by lower visibility and gradual incorporation of revenue sharing funds into the regular budget; fungibility; little increased local capacity to deal with local problems; little change in local budgetary processes; little citizen participation outside the large cities; little impact on government structure but interest in change. With these results in mind, let us now ask whether they can be used to enlighten the current debate over renewal of revenue sharing.

Proposals for Change

Formula

A variety of formula issues are under discussion, including eligibility, minimum payments, the appropriate state–local split, the appropriate floor and ceiling limits, and financial incentives for modernization. Given that the research reviewed here does not include formula research, it contributes little to our understanding of how the current formula or various formula changes might work. What it can offer is information on local and state officials' preferences regarding desirable directions for formula changes.

For example, except for officials in the small municipalities, substantial support can be found among both local and state officials for changes in the formula to encourage consolidation of the smallest units of local government. There is also substantial support for providing more funds to poor communities, although not for increasing funds to all large cities per se. Therefore, suggestions in the bills introduced by Representative Robert Drinan (H.R. 8329) and by Representative Dante Fascell (H.R. 10319) to raise the ceiling, drop the floor, impose a higher minimum payment, and allow intrastate allocations to reflect relative tax burdens of state and local government move in a direction likely to be well-received by many state and local officials. Proposals to help large cities explicitly rather than poor communities more generally are not likely to find much support.

In contrast to Drinan's and Fascell's proposals for change, the administration's bill (H.R. 8244) suggests no formula changes of consequence. It would gradually phase in a somewhat higher ceiling, a change that might be seen as a benefit to some poor communities, but no other changes are proposed.

Accountability and Autonomy

The administration has opposed the imposition of further restrictions on the way revenue sharing funds can be spent on the grounds that the program's major impact has been to increase the capacity of local governments to address locally defined problems. Two strings, priority categories and no-match, appear to inhibit local capacity. Even though these restrictions are difficult to enforce, many local officials seem to have been very cautious in using GRS funds for activities supported by other federal grants. Local and state officials would prefer a program without category and no-match restrictions, but none of the three proposals suggests omitting priority categories and only Fascell proposes eliminating no-match.

In fact, Drinan's bill proposes a tightening of the priority category restrictions in two ways: through maintenance of effort requirements and through requirements to spend a certain proportion of revenue sharing funds in various categories. The major purpose of these strings is to insure that local governments use funds to expand programs rather than to replace local funds or cut taxes. While the revenue sharing research speaks to this proposal only indirectly, its desirability and practicality seems questionable on other grounds.

The question of desirability is particularly troubling with regard to those programs Drinan especially wishes to safeguard—social service and health-care programs in large cities. Many of these cities, faced with escalating personnel and other costs and increasing demands for these services, are seeking alternatives to layoffs and reductions in service by attempting to share the costs of such services with other levels of government. A number of large cities, for example, are currently negotiating with state and county governments for the transfer of part or all of the responsibility for the operation of city hospitals. While such transfers may not diminish (and may even increase) the level of service to city residents, they may well result in substantial reductions in the dollar levels of city health accounts. To insist that such cities transfer dollars from other accounts in order to keep city health spending levels constant is of questionable desirability, particularly given the financial pressures that produced these transfers initially.

While this problem is particularly marked in large cities, it is by no means limited to them. Social service and health programs in most localities are administered through a complex network of state, county, city, and private agencies, using funds from a variety of sources. Changes in spending levels for any one of the governments involved may have no relationship to changes in service levels, but may reflect marginal adjustments in program responsibility, elimination of local salary supplements, or any of a variety of other administrative changes. To require that any government that finds itself spending less as the result of such changes transfer funds in order to continue to receive revenue sharing funds would complicate local accounting, but it is doubtful that it would, by itself, have the impact intended by the Drinan proposal.

Moreover, it seems unlikely that the maintenance of effort proposal will be successful in eliminating fungibility. Most accounts in most local units increase from year to year to accommodate inflation, salary increases, and changes in work load. Local officials could find accounts to support at the same level as last year, use revenue sharing funds to subsidize increases, and use the freed-up increment of funds elsewhere. Put another way, a local government can keep the dollar level in a particular account affected by revenue sharing the same, or even increase it; and still be substituting funds, since it might have used its own funds in place of some fraction of the revenue sharing funds had the program not been present. Detecting such practices, as the GAO has repeatedly insisted, requires an examination not only of the accounts allegedly affected by revenue sharing, but of the unit's entire revenue and expenditure pattern over a period of several years.[23]

Much the same difficulty seems apparent with regard to Drinan's attempt to prevent tax reduction. In spite of the publicity attached to the use of revenue sharing to cut taxes in some cities, most of the research summarized here reports that a relatively small percentage of revenue sharing funds have been used to cut taxes directly. Rather, revenue sharing's main impact on taxes seems to have taken the form of deferring increases, rather than direct reductions. This type of tax substitution is extremely difficult to detect and, like "fungibility," requires examination of revenue and expenditure patterns for a number of years.[24] While one can make a strong circumstantial case that a particular locality would have experienced a tax increase without revenue sharing, the absence of any solid accounting evidence would make withholding funds on these grounds extremely difficult.

At the same time that Drinan proposes tightening up accountability through restrictions, he also proposes expanding citizen input mechanisms. He would require the formation of citizen advisory committees, the appointment of citizen advocates to insure that citizen views are represented, and he would set aside a fraction of GRS appropriations to finance these efforts. Fascell's proposal would require public hearings, citizen advisory committees in larger jurisdictions, and extensive publication of budget documents.

However, providing opportunities for participation (e.g., hearings, advisory committees, advocates) will not insure that the interests of all citizens are expressed. In particular, it will not guarantee the participation of the poor. Recent studies of political participation have agreed that participators are not merely a representative sample of all citizens. Rather, participators tend to be wealthier, whiter, and more middled aged than the adult population as a whole. They also face problems and share views that are different from those of the nonparticipators in the population.[25] Evidence on citizen advisory committees convincingly argues that in the absence of federal requirements, official appointments to advisory committees do not include people who represent the full social, economic, and racial population of the locality.[f] On the other hand, if advisory committee members are elected rather than appointed, the elections are likely to be characterized by very low turnouts, allowing a few actives to control the results.[g]

While Drinan's proposal recognizes low levels of participation by citizens in general and by the poor in particular as problems, the suggestion offered is unlikely to solve either. There is no reason to expect citizen advocates to be any more effective in discerning citizen preferences than other mechanisms have been in the past. If advocates are hired by local officials, they are likely to follow the pattern of many model city directors, choosing "to maintain their identification with their city halls and negotiate at arm's length with neighborhood organizations."[26]

Advocates will advocate for city hall, or at best for those citizens who contact them. In most circumstances, this would give the floor to groups and individuals, already part of the ongoing political process. In addition, Drinan would require citizen advocates only in the largest localities, presumably in an effort to impact most of the GRS funds. However, as indicated above, the largest communities are the only ones in which mayors and county executives reported citizen interest, criticism, and attendance increases at hearings. These are also the communities that

---

[f] For early experience with Community Action and Model Cities, see James Sundquist, *Making Federalism Work* (Washington: Brookings Institution, 1969). For later experience with the planned variations version of model cities, see HUD "Planned Variations: First Year Survey," *Community Development Evaluation Series* (Washington: 1972).

[g] On low turnout in city elections generally, see Howard Hamilton, "The Municipal Voter: Voting and Non-Voting in City Elections," *American Political Science Review* 65 (1971), pp. 1135–40. On elections to CAA boards, see Eric Nordlinger and Jim Hardy, "Urban Decentralization," *Public Policy* 20 (summer 1972), p. 370.

already have hearings and advisory committees. Drinan's proposal would require an additional participation mechanism in just those places where above average participation already exists.

Richard P. Nathan has characterized the "basic philosophical issue" of the participation debate as "government *by representation* versus government *by participation*."[27] In fact, there is nothing in any of the proposals discussed here that would allow the citizenry to allocate funds or even force government leaders to act according to citizen preferences. What is desired is that representatives understand citizen preferences and seriously take them into account in making decisions. But there is no reason to believe that special GRS hearings, advisory committees, and advocates will achieve these goals.

In any case, there is a basic conflict between efforts to increase citizen input to revenue sharing decisions and those to increase restrictions on how funds are to be spent. The Drinan argument appears to assume that increased participation would result in further pressure to spend revenue sharing on social services. We have shown, however, that expanded citizen participation is associated with *lower* social service expenditures in counties. A fundamental conflict between restrictions and participation seems unavoidable: one can have local accountability or national standards, but apparently not both.

Another effort to increase accountability for federal funds can be seen in proposals for changing the appropriations process for GRS at the federal level. Both Drinan and Fascell move away from a single authorization and appropriation covering the entire life of the act. Drinan suggests a five-year authorization with annual appropriations. Fascell proposes an initial multiyear funding period followed by annual funding three years in advance. Given earlier evidence of the effects of uncertainty of funding on program expenditures, it seems that the Fascell suggestion is preferable unless high levels of capital outlays are judged to be desirable. It maintains an element of certainty in local budgeting by providing for a rolling appropriations process. While one would not expect major shifts to occur as a result of the Fascell bill, its appropriation provision should place operating expenditures on a more equal footing with less hazardous (e.g., capital expenditures) uses of the funds.

On the Adequacy of Evaluation Research

The research work relied on above represents an impressive effort, largely by academics, to apply their skills to evaluating a major public program. In spite of the quality of the researchers and the high level of support provided by the National Science Foundation and other funding sources, a number of major issues currently under debate are not addressed. For example, most of the work reviewed here devotes little attention to the civil rights issue that is so central to the discussion of GRS renewal. In spite of the GAO's persuasive argument that fungibility created considerable potential for governments to evade antidiscrimination statutes, we know relatively little about the extent to which local use of revenue sharing was constrained by compliance problems.[28] Nor does the research summarized above speak very eloquently to issues such as the use of revenue sharing as a countercyclical device, the potential impact of maintenance of effort, proposals to bypass state governments, or other similarly "hot" issues in the renewal debate. Furthermore, a number of the issues addressed are no longer of great concern. For example, considerable effort was made in the survey to assess official attitudes toward continuing the program and toward eliminating restrictions such as the priority categories—issues that no longer seem central. Since we believe strongly in the desirability of evaluation research, it is important to ask why so much that is relevant was left unattended while less relevant issues received the attention of well-trained and well-funded researchers.

One plausible answer arises from the fact that most of the researchers are academics, operating in academic settings. Individuals in such settings are seldom able to devote sufficient attention to the details of public policy, particularly if their disciplinary training emphasizes abstract rather than practical problem definitions. Although perfectly competent for academic pursuits, individual academics may exhibit what Veblen referred to as a "trained incapacity" to deal with a complex policy issue. Moreover, according to this argument academic techniques such as survey research are inherently inflexible: once questions have been formulated, research is too "locked in" to particular problem formulations and data needs to adapt to changes in the problems being studied or to recognize real world conditions that violate analytically convenient assumptions. If, from this point of view, important aspects of the revenue sharing problem were missed while less important aspects were studied, the most likely cause was the academics who did most of the work.

However plausible this explanation may appear, it overlooks two things. The first is the variety of techniques used to analyze the program's impact. While individual techniques may well be insensitive to major classes of impacts, much of what falls through the cracks of one approach may be picked up by another. Indeed, given the wide variety of methods used and situations studied, the degree of consensus on the general features of the impact of revenue sharing and the extent of complementarity is both surprising and reassuring

The charges of academic insensitivity and ignorance also overlook the influence exercised in many projects by practitioner-dominated advisory committees. The Michigan survey, for example, was assisted by an advisory committee compromising representatives from the Advisory Commission on Intergovernmental Relations, the Office of Revenue Sharing, the Office of Management and Budget, the Bureau of the Census, the General Accounting Office, and staff from the relevant congressional committees—not to mention the major public interest groups. Advisory committee members were active in the project from the beginning and exercised considerable influence over the number and type of questions to be asked, format, and sample design. While the academics may have indeed been ignorant of, and insensitive to, the "real world," people in the advisory committee were not. This first explanation, then, is unsatisfactory.[h]

An alternate and more persuasive explanation is that between 1974 and 1976, *the issue itself changed.* In mid-1974, when the bulk of the academic research was being organized, the "face" of the issue was defined by concern over the extent to which local and state officials supported the "new federalism" embodied in the program, the extent of which local governments would be revitalized by GRS dollars, and the uses of those dollars in local communities. By the fall of 1975 the last of these three concerns had been rethought and totally reformulated. Two persuasively argued reports by the General Accounting Office and the preliminary results from several academic studies showed that there was no way to discover the ultimate uses of revenue sharing dollars short of comprehensive information, over time, on all aspects of municipal budgets. Actual Use Reports could not be regarded as accurate, and only detailed study, municipality by municipality, could provide the necessary information. A few of these intensive studies were undertaken, but the techniques required could not feasibly be applied to large numbers of recipient jurisdictions. The question had been usefully reformulated from a concern with the stated uses of revenue sharing dollars to concern with fiscal effects of the program. The question was better, but answers became more difficult to obtain.

Further, a high rate of inflation and the widely publicized financial pressure on many large cities effectively undermined the significance of the "revitalization" and "support" issues. Rather than provide funds for innovations or new programs, revenue sharing increasingly provided funds seen as necessary just to maintain existing services. Public interest groups, which had earlier pressed for liberalization of the program and

---

[h] While insensitivity to the "real world" was not an advisory committee problem, other problems did hinder the effectiveness of the advisory committee setup. Discussion of these is important but beyond the scope of our present effort.

expansion of its appropriations, became increasingly willing to settle for an extension of the program rather than jeopardize its continuation. The renewal of the program, problematic in 1974, had become much more certain by mid-1975. Attention shifted accordingly to a new set of issues, more appropriate for the changed context, but largely outside the purview of researchers intent on evaluating an outmoded definition of the problem.

Over this period, the political lines of division over what form the program should take changed as well. As recently as January of 1975, a no-strings program appeared feasible. The concept had been endorsed by most of the major public interest groups and recommended by the administration's Revenue Sharing Study Group.[29] Between the Study Group Report in January and the introduction of the administration bill in April, however, it became apparent that this version of the program was politically indefensible. The program had come under increasing attack from congressional liberals, who charged that too much revenue sharing had been used to cut taxes, and that "fungibility" removed any possibility of holding local officials accountable for how funds were spent. In addition, many civil rights groups, which had earlier favored the abolition of revenue sharing in favor of the expansion of categorical programs, seem to have become aware of the program's potential for bringing hitherto unregulated governments and programs under the influence of federal antidiscrimination statutes. These groups were prepared to support renewal, but only under vastly different circumstances. In this political climate, a no-strings program was exceedingly difficult to defend. Accordingly, this alternative, together with much research that supported it, was discarded.

That issues change their significance over time, and that political forces limit the range of feasible alternatives, are hardly novel observations. Their crucial impact on the "relevance" of research work, however, can easily be overlooked in the rush to complete research reports in time to be thought useful. If policy issues do change their significance and their politics over time, the immediate relevance of research results is likely to be purely accidental. Only by predicting issues and political divisions in advance can research be "relevant" when produced, but even the practitioners on the advisory committees were unable to do that.

Arguing that academic research is seldom likely to be directly "relevant" does not suggest that we abolish academic evaluation. Rather, both scholars and practitioners should realize that governmental organizations have different types of information needs and that academics can reasonably meet only some of these needs. The revenue sharing experience suggests that academic research is not well-suited to providing judgments about the administrative feasibility or the political consequences of the details of particular program options. It can, however, usefully address questions of more lasting significance within a policy area and identify issues that require further attention.

The GRS research, for example, reported a number of findings of considerable significance for intergovernmental grants policy. The research made clear that efforts to assess the impact of any single source of revenue, without consideration of other available funds, is bound to be meaningless. Further, the Michigan study pointed out important differences between small and large cities, between cities and counties, among localities in various regions of the country, and between the perspectives of local executives and finance officers. These differences add important qualifiers to case studies and fragmentary information. They point to missing information that may substantially alter one's perspective. Indeed, the shaping of more accurate perspectives on state and local fiscal behavior may be the most important long-term contribution to policy making made by the various research reports.

Notes

1. F. Thomas Juster, ed., *The Economic and Political Impact of General Revenue Sharing* (Washington: U.S. Government Printing Office, forthcoming).

2. Richard Nathan et al., *Monitoring Revenue Sharing* (Washington: Brookings Institution, 1974).

3. Gail Wilensky, "Modelling the Fiscal Impact of Revenue Sharing," in Juster, *Impact of Revenue Sharing,* pp. 2–3.

4. F. Thomas Juster, "Program Impact of Revenue Sharing," in Juster, *Impact of Revenue Sharing.*

5. Nathan et al., *Monitoring Revenue Sharing,* pp. 266–74.

6. See Thomas Anton et al., *Understanding the Fiscal Impact of General Revenue Sharing* (Ann Arbor: Institute for Public Policy Studies, 1975), pp. 98–103; Nathan et al., *Monitoring Revenue Sharing,* pp. 229–30; Wilensky, "Modeling the Fiscal Impact of Revenue Sharing," pp. 23–24.

7. James Fossett, "GRS and Decision Making in Local Government," in Juster, *Impact of Revenue Sharing,* pp. 29–32.

8. Comptroller General, *Revenue Sharing: Its Use and Impact on Local Governments,* (Washington: Government Printing Office, 1974), pp. 29–33.

9. Fossett, "GRS and Decision Making in Local Government," p. 40.

10. Edie Goldenberg, "Citizen Participation in General Revenue Sharing," in Juster, *Impact of Revenue Sharing,* pp. 6 and 12.

11. Fossett, "GRS and Decision Making in Local Government," pp. 37, 62–63.

12. Nathan et al., *Monitoring Revenue Sharing,* pp. 202–4.

13. See particularly John P. Crecine, *Governmental Problem Solving* (Skokie: Rand-McNally, 1969), p. 74.

14. See Wilensky, "Modelling the Fiscal Impact," and Nathan et al., *Monitoring Revenue Sharing,* pp. 229–30.

15. Opinion Research Corporation, *The General Public and Community Leaders View the General Revenue Sharing Program* (Princeton, N.J.: January 1975), pp. 30–31.

16. Steven A. Waldhorn et al., *Planning and Participation: General Revenue Sharing in Ten Large Cities* (Menlo Park, California: Stanford Research Institute, August, 1975), p. 14.

17. Goldenberg, "Citizen Participation," pp. 18–19, 26–29.

18. Ibid., pp. 22–23.

19. Ibid, pp. 48–51. Also see Richard L. Cole, "Revenue Sharing: Citizen Participation and Social Service Aspects," *The Annals of the American Academy of Political and Social Science* 419 (May 1975), pp. 63–74.

20. Goldenberg, "Citizen Participation," pp. 24, 45–48.

21. Thomas Anton, "General Revenue Sharing and State–Local Government Structure," in Juster, *Impact of Revenue Sharing,* pp. 18–19.

22. Anton, "General Revenue Sharing," pp. 22–24.

23. Comptroller General, *Use and Impact on Local Governments and 26 Cities,* (Washington: Government Printing Office, 1974).

24. Nathan et al., *Monitoring Revenue Sharing,* p. 199; Lovell, *The Effects of General Revenue Sharing,* pp. 47–48. See also Comptroller General, *Use and Impact on Local Governments and 26 Cities,* pp. 10–15.

25. Sidney Verba and Norman Nie, *Participation in America* (New York: Harper & Row, 1972) pp. 125–37, 267–85.

26. James Sundquist, *Making Federalism Work,* (Washington: Brookings Institution, 1969), p. 97.

27. Testimony before Subcommittee on Intergovernmental Relations of House Committee on Government Operations, October 2, 1975.

28. Comptroller General, *Use and Impact on Local Governments of 26 Cities,* p. 35.

29. Joel Havemann, "Ford to recommend few changes in Revenue Sharing," *National Journal* (January 1975), pp. 85–92 and Idem, "Last Minute Extension of Revenue Sharing Expected," *National Journal* (August 8, 1975), pp. 1140–45.

6

NSF-sponsored Research on General Revenue Sharing: The Formula

Trudi Miller Lucas

The Research Applications Directorate (RANN) of the National Science Foundation supported a $3,000,000 research program on general revenue sharing. The program was something of an adventure for NSF, because it threw the foundation, with its commitment to science, in the middle of a salient and important political debate. On one hand, RANN had to support social scientific projects that met the foundation's standards of rigor and quality. On the other, it had to get results that would be useful in partisan deliberations over the renewal of revenue sharing.

It is too soon to assess the impact of the research on the decision-making process. The experimental intervention—the research program itself—has not run its course. The results of Michigan's large survey of state and local officials are still in preliminary form.[1] Also, the last dissemination project on the formula—one that answers decision maker's questions directly—has just been launched.[2] Most importantly, the event to be influenced, the final decision on revenue sharing, has not occurred.

While we cannot describe the impact of the program on the decision-making process, we can describe the design of the program, which should be interesting to readers who are concerned about methodological issues. In the following sections we cover first the tensions that developed among considerations of scientific objectivity, politics, and methods in the design of the program. We then describe the research program for the formula that was developed to resolve those tensions. For readers not altogether comfortable with their grasp of the algorithm, there is an appendix after the conclusion, which covers briefly the workings of the present formula.

The author is an employee of NSF/RANN and had daily responsibility for the revenue sharing research program. The opinions expressed in this chapter are solely those of the author and do not necessarily reflect those of NSF/RANN.

109

Politics, Objectivity, and Scientific Methods

One of RANN's functions is to bridge the gap between the worlds of policy and research. This mission is complicated by the apparent incompatability between the needs of the users for very specific information about the winners and losers and the desire of social scientists to rise above special interests in a value-free quest for information. Bridging the gap is further complicated by the difficulty of purging values from social science research. Indeed, we argue that it is unlikely that simplifying assumptions necessary for the conduct of empirical inquiries can be made without introducing partisan biases. These points are developed below.

The stakes in the politics of general revenue sharing are high. They were high when the act was passed in 1972, and they are high again as renewal is considered before expiration in December 1976. Diverse groups are affected. In the first place there are the chief executives and other officials of the 38,000 general-purpose governments eligible for funds. Their interests, which are not altogether compatable or equally intense, are represented by various organizations, for example, the League of Cities, the Conference of Mayors, the National Conference of State Legislatures, the National Governors Conference, the National Association of Counties, the International City Managers Association, the American Federation of State, County and Municipal Employees, the Municipal Finance Officers Association, and the National Association of Regional Councils. Also interested, because of the amount of funds (about $6 billion a year) and because GRS competes with other programs, are the nongovernment public and special interest groups. Again, these groups have varying concerns and intensity of concerns about GRS. They include the League of Women Voters, the NAACP, the Southern Regional Council, the National Urban Coalition, the National Urban League, the National Center for Urban Ethnic Affairs, Common Cause, the American Friends Committee, the AFL–CIO, YMCA National Boards, United Methodist Church, National Conference on Catholic Charities, National Council of Jewish Women, National Council on the Aging, National Association of Social Workers, Lawyers Committee for Civil Rights Under Law, Americans for Democratic Action, and many others. In spite of the number of legislative issues affecting their constituencies, most of these groups listed have conducted their own studies and prepared reports on general revenue sharing.

Organized political actors with stakes in the general revenue sharing program also include individual members of Congress and, of course, the congressional committees responsible for primary deliberation on renewal. These groups have also been involved in the conduct of original and major studies on GRS. Deeply involved are the Office of Revenue Sharing, Treasury, the Office of Management and Budget, and the Bureau of the Census. Most mission agencies, for example, Agriculture, HUD, HEW, DOL, have at least one staff person keeping current on aspects of the program. Political actors also include members of Congress who have constituents diversely affected by the program, some more saliently than others. Finally, both GAO and the Advisory Commission on Intergovernmental Relations have expended thousands of hours of staff time studying general revenue sharing.

As the partial list of groups engaged with GRS indicates, the field of political actors is diverse. Each group is concerned about outcomes or dependent variables of importance to them, for example, extent of citizen participation and civil rights compliance, levels of program funds, the simplification of federal programs, government solvency, or personnel practices. Each is disposed to oppose or support features of the GRS program because of connections assumed between program features and outcomes of interest.

The orientation toward research results on the part of political actors seems to vary inversely with the certainty with which connections between policy instruments (program features) and salient outcomes can be assumed. Where actors are uncertain of important connections, they want information. They may not act on the information because of other priorities, but they do want the information.

Unlike the major political actors, the National Science Foundation as an institution does not have a stake in the policy outcomes of debates over general revenue sharing. The foundation is not a mission agency with responsibility for the program to be evaluated. This independence increases RANN's capacity for funding objective assessments of current programs and problems. In addition, the foundation's major constituents are academics who have historically maintained their independence from vested and special interests. Institutionally, then, RANN should be more oriented to objectivity in applied research than most offices that support it. Indeed, the commitment of NSF/RANN to objectivity and independence from political considerations made the decision to launch a large program on GRS difficult.

Objectively in research is supposed to be produced through the application of scientific methods. For revenue sharing, the social scientific tools are found primarily in the disciplines of economics, public administration, law, sociology, and psychology. Unfortunately the methods employed by these disciplines can mix technical or methodological decisions with political values and assumptions; for example, the choice of subjects for study may determine answers, the causal arrow in a model may establish blame, the theory of a discipline may lead to a focus on certain policy variables rather than others, or theory may lead to a focus on nonpolicy variables and the conclusion that social problems are intractable. To be more specific for the case of general revenue sharing, the following are examples of methodological questions that can influence or bias findings politically.

1. How large should a study of opinions on GRS be? It simply is not possible economically to do a survey that will produce adequate samples of all possible interest groups for separate analysis. Therefore, dissenting opinions of some groups—most likely minorities or less powerful groups—can be ignored or underrepresented.

2. How should the responses of groups included in a survey be weighted? If one wants to tell national decision makers about the national effects of the revenue sharing program, one might weight the responses of public officials (or others) representing the receipt of the largest numbers of revenue sharing dollars more heavily. However, the interests of individuals in large places may differ dramatically from those in small places. Which represents bias—weighting by dollars or not weighting by dollars?

3. Should one use financial data or survey data to determine the impact of GRS on the structure of local governments? If one only uses the financial data (e.g., census of governments data) one may falsely conclude that the program provides no incentives for structural change in local government. Local officials may be waiting to see if features, like the definition of adjusted taxes in the formula, will change. If one only uses survey data one may pick up false assumptions that good things (or bad things) will result from a program that is liked (or disliked) for other reasons. The probability of finding changes associated with the program varies predictably with the choice of method, in part, simply because financial data are likely to be older.

4. Can one design a formula that better allocates money according to need? There are at least three families of need indexes. The first has to do with population income, the second has to do with the burden of services carried by governments, the third has to do with fiscal capacity—broadly defined as the governments' ability to meet constituency requirements. Moreover, within this third family, constituency requirements can be defined normatively in terms of desirable or average levels of service, or empirically as the level of services a jurisdiction actually provides. Similarly fiscal ability can be measured by per-capita income, indexes of poverty, revenue collected, or revenue expected if average tax rates are imposed. In other words, the result of operationalizing a popular formula change "to target money on governments with the greatest needs" will depend largely on the definition and indexes of need.

The above list just samples areas where technical decisions forced on the research by the need to keep the study "doable" may influence findings in a politically sensitive way. It does not even touch on the problems of direction of causation, multicolinearity, different levels of aggregation in the data base, or assumptions about equation form. Hopefully, however, this list plus the other discussions in this volume convey the obvious message that simplifying assumptions, which are unavoidable in the conduct of empirical studies, do have their counterparts in the beliefs and goals of political actors. Potentially, then social scientific studies can produce results that give one political actor an advantage over another, although the data do not unambiguously support the conclusions. Indeed, given the necessity of making simplifying assumptions and the diversity of political actors with high stakes in the policy questions, some political bias in studies is unavoidable.

The high probability of unintended bias in social scientific research on general revenue sharing spelled potential trouble for RANN in dealing with both the intended users of research and the scientific community. Users who discovered research results that contradicted firmly held beliefs could challenge these studies as biased. Verified findings of bias confirm the fears of academics that applied social science is inadequately objective.

The Research Program

The research program on general revenue sharing met the problems head on. The research, especially on the formula, was overtly and deliberately oriented toward gauging effects on partisan policy objectives. For example, people who defined the need for GRS in terms of population poverty were given a critique of the formula from that perspective and an alternative formula that distributed more money to governments with high concentrations of poor people. The research program as a whole, however, adopted an objective or nonpartisan stance by trying to represent the total array of special interests. Also, the results of the studies were synthesized into one volume so that the decision maker who represented the "public" interest, that is, the combination or sum of special interests, could study a full range of policy options and their effects on specific policy objectives and special interests.

In the following paragraphs the research program is described first as a set of assumptions or an abstract model, and then briefly as an operating program that extended over a period of two years. The model, developed in part from hindsight, was most clearly realized for research on the allocation formula.

The research program design was based in part on the assumption that policy questions are about the effects of policies on interest groups and their articulated preferences. Conceptually the GRS user or interest group listed above can be strung along a continuum from occupation with a narrow constituency to concern about all domestic constituencies. Some user groups focus on an array of constituents as well as the array of policy instruments and ask now can we maximize winners and minimize losers across the nation? This latter decision maker has the "public" interest in mind, which we define as an aggregation of narrow interests.

For the development of useful research products, we assume that decision makers representing both special and "public" or "national" interests want information about winners and losers. Special interests want information about effects of policies on their constituencies first. They also want to know effects on other constituencies because they need to build coalitions. Therefore special interests should be satisfied if policy research yields a "position paper" that provides information about a policy's effect on them, and information about whom they should work with to maximize their interest vis-à-vis that policy. National decision makers in turn want information about effects on all interest groups so they can implement policies that do the greatest good for the greatest number of people. What they want from policy research is an "option paper" that arrays all feasible decision alternatives and indicates their effects on major constituencies. This option paper should allow them to identify the "public" interest.

The assumption that policy questions are about effects on constituents leads to a second assumption that the demand for policy research should go up when connections between policy instruments and interests are complex. The formula is a good example. Even people who have been working with the formula for years argue they cannot predict what types of governments among the 38,000 will win or lose as a result of most formula changes. The formula, written out, is six feet long; yet, it can't be used to calculate allocations to a single government without running a whole state. If special interest groups or national decision makers want to change the formula to achieve a better distribution from their perspective, they need access to the algorithm, appropriate data tapes, software to summarize distributional patterns (unless they represent a single government) and, if they want to keep running costs within limits, a big computer.

The design for the research program was also based on the assumption that it is virtually impossible to design objective, nonpartisan empirical studies. Current practice among social science researchers acknowledges this fact. Simplification of assumptions creates a framework within which study results must be interpreted. Framework is another word for point of view, and a point of view created by technical–methodological decisions does have partisan content. It is true that such a perspective is not usually overtly partisan. Rather it is composed of a jumble of decisions about sample selections, variable inclusion, causality, equation form, and other research design choices that probably do not add up to a political position. Nevertheless, empirical researchers rarely claim they have tested all points of view or that their results can be generalized beyond the limits established by simplifying assumptions. Indeed, the progress in objective, scientific, empirical research seems to be toward increasing care in narrowing perspectives, especially in reporting results. In other words, "objective" as an adjective before research does not in practice mean "comprehensive" or "without a point of view." Rather, operationally, it means research conducted from a point of view that is clearly communicated so that no one is fooled about where and how the findings apply.

Given the inevitability of some partisan bias in individual research projects, objectivity in a research program may be maximized by making partisan assumptions overt for each study while covering all major partisan positions in the program's aggregation of study. To achieve this sort of democratic or multipartisan objectivity, many questions have to be answered for each of the stake-holder groups. How does each group define its goals and interests? What assumptions do they make about the connection among these interests, existing institutions, the interests of other groups in society, and the potentials of man and society for reform? Do these assumptions and other untested philosophical assumptions have counterparts in technical–methodological decisions such as those about equation form, direction of causality, or variables that will be included in the model? How does each partisan group define highly valued but diffuse concepts such as equal opportunity, representative democracy, and deprivation? How well do these definitions fit with proxies and operational definitions used in analysis?

With answers to these questions, one could crudely estimate the amount of bias associated with proposed studies and make decisions about requirements for alternative models and different data sets to insure a nonpartisan (or multipartisan) perspective in the research program. One could also deliberately design a representative array of partisan studies that employed the assumptions of each partisan group where assumptions must be made to execute a quantitative study.

A program that efficiently answered these questions and represented as many of the extremely contrasting perspectives as funds allowed could, in the ideal, be as multipartisan or public spirited as our representative–democratic system. Indeed, in theory, it could be more representative since it could "overrepresent" the interests of less powerful groups in society.

We further assume that a multipartisan research program would meet the needs of decision makers representing special interests and the public interest by providing information for position and option papers. The partisan would have an analysis of the policy issue that focused on his problem and did not make any simplifying assumptions he would disagree with. This would give him the vital part of his position paper. In addition, however, he would want general information about groups who won when he did and lost when he did so that he could establish coalitions. For this he would probably want a synthesis of findings that covered the full array of studies. This synthesis would also serve as the public interest decision maker's option paper.

Ideally, the synthesis would lay out the partisan implications of the assumptions of all studies, and establish ranges of effects that would hold up statistically regardless of assumptions. If these ranges were large, results would show that the public interest could not be established through research. However, results displayed in the synthesis could still be useful in the decision process because each partisan group should have better information about how specific policy or program features relate to its interest. If ranges were small, that is, if many partisan research projects pointed toward the desirability of a given policy position, the decision maker speaking for the public should be able to establish a policy position from the synthesis.

We thus assume that a research program structured along overtly partisan lines would keep both RANN's constituents happy. The users would have relevant and reliable information about winners and losers. The academics would have an approach to the conduct of policy research that was wholly consistent with the requirements of good social science. Indeed, turning the spotlight on the partisan implications of standard methodological approaches could lead to a significant advance in the quality of basic research.

One last assumption entered into the design of the revenue sharing research program that was peculiar to that particular policy issue. Revenue sharing was coming up for renewal shortly, and we assumed we would have only about a year and a half to get results. This, combined with our interest in tackling the complex research questions, made it necessary to divide the programs' total work load into many small independent studies.

Table 6–1 summarizes our assumptions in program design.

The abstract model of a research program outlined above was not fully or precisely applied. We came closest to it for research on the formula. The series of tasks involved in executing the research program on the formula were to (1) identify interest group concerns about the formula, (2) identify the existing research, (3) provide the research tools

Table 6–1
GRS Research Program Assumptions

It Is Assumed That:	Decision Maker Has:	
	Single Constituency	All Constituencies
D.M.'s interest is	partisan	public
The policy goal is	to maximize constituency benefit	to do the greatest good for the greatest number
The research should produce	a position paper (including synthesis information)	an option paper synthesizing positions
The demand for policy research is greater when	it is hard to .identify winners and losers	it is hard to identify winners and losers
The time for getting GRS results in the proper form is	short	too short[a]
The responsibility for multipartisan representation rests with	the principal investigator or researcher	RANN

[a] The decision on GRS is at least a half year behind schedule. We wouldn't have been able to produce the synthesis in time if it weren't late.

required for independent study of the formula, (4) identify performers, (5) monitor the research, (6) evaluate the individual research reports, (7) synthesize research across formula issues and critiques, and (8) get the results to the people who had to make the policy decisions.

The first two needs were met primarily through a grant to the National Planning Association to prepare a bibliography, a compendium of research in progress, and a paper on the issues surrounding the passage and implementation of GRS.[3] NPA also hosted a conference on General Revenue Sharing that brought together researchers from many disciplines who might be expected to know about revenue sharing and representatives of the policy community or "users" (e.g., staff from the executive branch and congressional committees, the public interest groups, and state and local governments).[4] At the conference (which was designed in consultation with a steering committee of users) researchers and policy makers were assigned to workshops. Some of these were on policy instruments (that is features of the existing law including one on the formula). Others were on expected impacts of the program. Participants in the "independent" or policy variable workshops were asked to predict impacts; participants in the dependent variable workshops were asked to identify causes. All were asked to identify problems in terms of data availability and research methods.

Analysis of workshop notes indicated that the formula was expected to have impacts on several of the outcome variables, and that it was a significant and controversial feature of the program. We also learned that we would have to do some tool building before we could support extensive research on the subject. First, we had to get Treasury's procedures for allocating funds, that is, the operational formula, into the public domain. Second, to eliminate redundancy and get a head start on data tape acquisition, we would have to merge 1972 Census of Government tapes, 1970 Census of Population and Housing tapes, and ORS data elements and output tapes.

If John Parker and others at ORS had not been extremely helpful, NSF would probably not have had a significant formula research program because of time constraints. Fortunately, the Office of Revenue Sharing was willing to assist Westat in the preparation of a fully documented and operational replica of their program for allocating shared revenue.[a] This product made research on the existing formula outside of government possible. ORS also did what it could to help DUALabs acquire and merge the necessary data tapes.[b]

Simultaneously, RANN designed a solicitation for formula research that identified eight goals for the formula. These goals or objectives reflected criticisms of the legislative history. The solicitation emerged as a call for advocacy research to identify faults in the existing formula from the perspective of different distributional objectives and to correct those faults through the design of new formula.[5]

Our major decision in the design of the solicitation was whether interest groups who do have research capabilities should be allowed to

---

[a] Program tapes are available from Westat, Inc. The following texts were also prepared under the award: "Overview of Distribution of Revenue Sharing Funds" (Rockville, Md.: Westat, Inc., 1974); "Documentation of Interstate Allocation Program" (Rockville, Md: Westat, Inc., 1974); "Documentation of the Computer Runs which Edit and Sort the Census Bureau Revenue Sharing Data Elements Master File" (Rockville, Md.: Westat, Inc., 1974); "Documentation of Intrastate Allocation Program" (Rockville, Md.: Westat, Inc., 1974); "Congressional and Administrative Rationale for the General Revenue Sharing Allocation Procedure" (Rockville, Md.: Westat, Inc., 1974).

[b] Files and documentation made available at cost through DUALabs, Rosslyn, Va. under the award are listed below. DUALabs maintains the capability to merge these files: 1967 Census of Governments Employment File; 1972 Census of Governments Finance File; 1970 Census Fourth Count/Revenue Sharing "MINI" File; 1972 Census of Governments Name and Address File; 1973 Fiscal Revenue Sharing Detailed Tas Data File; 1970 Census Fourth Count/Revenue Sharing "MAXI" File.

compete for research grants. Our decision was negative. Instead, and unfortunately belatedly, these groups were included in the circle of executive branch and congressional staff users who reviewed drafts of the solicitation. Through this circulation to users we attempted to augment and refine information on the importance of formula issues to the array of interest groups.

From the perspective of policy research, the process by which the program was designed had yielded a separation of value questions from technical questions. Distributional goals or political positions on what the formula should do had been identified before the research began — hopefully in a manner that assured proper representation of all stakeholder groups. Thesefore, researchers were not cast in the inappropriate role of defining "fair" or "good" distributions. The research in turn was focused on if not limited to the technical or research question of how a given distributional goal could be achieved. The resultant research was intended to be both overtly political and blandly scientific. On the political side advocates were being given advice on how they could achieve their policy goals by manipulating the formula. On the research side, activities were focused on factual questions.

Seven awards were made under the solicitation for formula research.[c] Before the solicitation came out RANN funded two special studies of alternative formula.[d] Monitoring these awards involved evaluation of preliminary reports and exhortation to finish final reports on time. For researchers funded under the solicitation, getting results on schedule required extraordinary effort. (Awards were mostly made in December 1974, and final reports were due June 15, 1975.) In spite of the difficulty, with one exception, the researchers funded under the solicitation were ready to testify before the Joint Economic Committee, June 17, 1975, two days after turning in their final reports.

----

[c] The research reports resulting from awards under the solicitation are listed below. Except for the Rand study, all are complete: Stephen M. Barro, "Equalization and Equity in General Revenue Sharing: An Analysis of Alternative Distribution Formulas" (Santa Monica, Calif.: Rand, 1975); Barry Jesmer et al., "General Revenue Sharing: Designing a formula which does not Discourage or Distort Local Variations in Financing and Delivering Services" (Rochester, N.Y.: Center for Governmental Research, Inc., 1975); Morton Lustig and Lawrence W. Garrtee, "Alternative Formula for General Revenue Sharing: Stability of Allocation, Part I and Part II" (Philadelphia, Pa.: University of Pennsylvania, 1975); John P. Ross et al., "Alternative Formulae for General Revenue Sharing: Population Based Measures of Need" (Blacksburg, Va.: Virginia Polytechnic Institute and State University, 1975); Gregory Schmid et al., "An Alternative Approach to General Revenue Sharing: A Needs-Based Allocation Formula" (Menlo Park, Calif.: Institute for the Future, 1975); G. Ross Stephens and Gerald W. Olson, "State Responsibility for Public Services and General Revenue Sharing" (Kansas City, Mo.: University of Missouri, 1975); Reese C. Wilson et al., "General Revenue Sharing Formula Alternatives" (Menlo Park, Calif.: Stanford Research Institute, 1975).

[d] One grant went to Robert Strauss, an important figure in the design of the original formula.

Following RANN policy, each final research report was evaluated by representatives of the technical or scientific community and by users. The American Statistical Association selected the technical evaluators. The major user evaluators were public interest groups representing governments, and organizations concerned primarily with citizen participation and civil rights—two areas where the GRS program had been challenged. Staff in the executive branch and congressional committees were invited to comment.

The synthesis effort for the formula took place in two stages. The first was an analysis of the texts and the evaluation of the reports.[6] The primary purpose was to discover features of the formula that seemed to warrant change regardless of the policy goal that drove the research. The second is an analysis of the output or distribution tapes from each formula project (about 15 different formulae overall) using a common analytic or descriptive package.[7] This data tape synthesis project will also design and describe formula changes recommended in several different projects focusing on different policy goals. It will, in other words, stress formula changes that should be popular across partisan perspectives.

Dissemination of the research results has taken many forms. Most obviously, final reports, summaries of reports, and snythesis volumes were mailed to individuals (primarily staff) in the interest groups, Congress, the executive branch, the major governmental interest groups (GAO, ACIR, CBO) evaluating revenue sharing, state and local governments, and the research community.

NSF also supported Stanford Research Institute in the production of an *Ancilla to Revenue Sharing Research*.[8] This volume expands the subject and name indexes and covers the original formula reports and other major research efforts as well as the SRI syntheses. This elaborate index should allow users to cover the literature on an existing formula feature or a proposed change quickly or thoroughly.

During the period when the volumes were being prepared and mailed, researchers were also presenting their results in person to users, for example, testimony before the Joint Economic Committee. The final dissemination effort is based on the data tape synthesis project and is

---

Robert P. Strauss, "The Impact of Alternative Interpretation of the Floor and Ceiling Provisions of the State and Local Fiscal Assistance Act of 1972" (Chapel Hill, N.C.: University of North Carolina, 1975).

A second went to the Brookings Institution to test out Brookings recommendations made in: Richard P. Nathan, Allen D. Manvel, and Susannah E. Calkins, *Monitoring Revenue Sharing* (Washington, D.C.: Brookings Institution, 1975).

The first formula report is available. The full report is to be published shortly. Richard P. Nathan and Jacob M. Jaffe, "Effects of the Statutory Formula Alternatives Section 108(c)(1), Brookings Studies of Revenue Sharing Alternatives, First Report" (Washington, D.C.: Brookings Institution, 1975).

intended to provide telephone answers to questions about the feasibility and probable effects of formula changes.[9]

Conclusion

The research program demonstrated that it is technically feasible to change the formula to better achieve diverse policy objectives, and broad dissemination of the research should extend competence to deal with formula issues beyond just a handful of experts in government. Without the research program, only groups who could get access to Treasury's computer system through ORS or the congressional committees could try their hand at formula engineering. Now, an interest group with $3,000 to $5,000 can run a simple formula change for the nation. Anyone can read the literature and decision makers have access to the telephone answering service. In short, the extention of knowledge about this highly complex policy instrument should contribute to the rationality and openness of the decision-making process.

Research on the formula has not yet produced clear guidance for the formulation of coalitions or the identification of the "public" or "national" interest. We have found some features of the formula that are problematic from the perspective of most of our studies, for example, the rigid one-third/two-thirds split between state and local governments and the application of the 145 percent limit—but there is as yet no clear consensus on how these features could be altered to gain the support of a coalition or perhaps a majority of interest groups.

Before the program has run its course, however, the data tape synthesis effort may identify specific changes that could be endorsed from many different political perspectives. These will probably be moderate in their impact. One example might be an alteration of the adjusted tax measure to reduce the penalty for governments who use user charges and nontax mechanisms to gather revenues. A change in the mechanism for limiting allocations in a multiplicative formula (a switch to something beside the 145% per-capita limit) might also appear beneficial to many interest groups. A reduced, lower (20%) per-capita limit is another possibility, as is a reduction in the 50 percent budget constraint. An alteration of the layering sequence to increase the equality of allocations going to governments with similar characteristics may also seem desirable. As these frequently suggested formula changes are described using criteria that are meaningful to the diverse interest groups, changes that could be endorsed by a winning political coalition may emerge. On the other hand, changes that are attractive to a majority may have little effect. They may not be worth the cost and effort of launching a coalition for formula alteration.

We can also report that to our knowledge, accusations that RANN has produced a politically biased set of findings have not emerged from the user community. There may be charges of bias from the academic community, perhaps in this book; if so, they will probably be about research on the processes and impacts of GRS, where we were unable to develop a tightly structured multipartisan program of research. Hopefully, also, the bias will be discovered in individual projects where it was anticipated and where compensation was achieved for the program as a whole. (For example, Michigan's survey is biased toward favorable views of GRS since only generalist officials were interviewed. However, department heads at the state and local level were studied separately by Deil S. Wright and Steven A. Waldhorn and the opinions of all groups are displayed together in the synthesis.)[10]

Readers who are interested by RANN's attempt to achieve objectivity through the systematic representation opposing partisan perspectives should note APRT's recent program solicitation for *Applied Research on the Benefits and Costs of Public Regulation*.[11] After a data-gathering phase, this solicitation calls for analysis of the costs and benefits of regulation in very sensitive areas. It requires that proposals "identify and include the significant divergent viewpoints on regulation of the commodity of service in question, e.g., those of industry, labor, public interest groups, and government organizations who have a significant involvement in the manufacture, distribution or regulation of the commodity." It also says "researchers performing these analyses will represent the divergent positions concerning the benefits and costs of regulation."

The solicitation seems to be evoking a favorable reaction from the Washington policy community, which is not surprising since it was designed with staff participation. The approach should also please academics advocating the use of sensitivity analysis, alternative models, and the accumulation of studies before findings are proclaimed.

Interestingly, the regulation solicitation was developed by economists (the present writer is a political scientist) independently of the general revenue sharing research program. Yet, it operationalizes the general model developed in the beginning of the previous section, except that responsibility for producing the option paper for determining the public interest is delegated to the research team. We might tentatively hypothesize that pressure from RANN's two constituency groups— academics and users—evokes an approach to social science independent of discipline or policy issue. The combined academic–user pressure says: "Hit the relevant political issues, but make sure you've tested the major alternative models before you state any findings." The resultant approach may not produce many recommendations for major changes pursuant of

123

the "public" interest, nevertheless, its basic intellectual honesty should appeal to both philosophers of science and hard-nosed public policy makers who are tired to being mislead by social scientists.

Notes

1. F. Thomas Juster et al., "A Survey of the Impact of General Revenue Sharing" (Washington, D.C.: U.S. Government Printing Office, forthcoming 1976).

2. Continuation: Grant APR-755247 A02.

3. Martharose F. Laffey, "General Revenue Sharing: A Bibliography" (Washington, D.C.: The National Planning Association, 1974), "Compendium of Revenue Sharing Research in Progress" (Washington, D.C.: The National Planning Association, 1974), and "Political Perspectives on General Revenue Sharing" (Washington, D.C.: The National Planning Association, 1974).

4. See "Proceedings of the Conference on Revenue Sharing" (Washington, D.C.: The National Planning Association, 1974).

5. *Program Solicitation: Alternative Formulae for General Revenue Sharing* (Washington, D.C.: NSF/RANN, 1974).

6. *General Revenue Sharing Research Utilization Program,* 5 volumes (Washington, D.C.: U.S. Government Printing Office, 1975).

7. Continuation: Grant APR-755247 A02.

8. *General Revenue Sharing Research Utilization Project, Volume 5, Ancilla to Revenue Sharing Research* (Washington, D.C.: U.S. Government Printing Office, 1975).

9. Continuation: Grant APR-755247 A02.

10. F. Thomas Juster et al., "A Survey of the Impact of General Revenue Sharing" (Washington, D.C.: U.S. Government Printing Office, forthcoming 1976); Diel S. Wright et al., "Assessing the Impacts of General Revenue Sharing in the Fifty States: A Survey of State Administrators" (Chapel Hill, N.C.: University of North Carolina, 1975); Steven A. Waldhorn, "Planning and Participation: General Revenue Sharing in Ten Large Cities" (Menlo Park, Calif.: Stanford Research Institute, 1975); *General Revenue Sharing Research Utilization Program, Volume IV, Synthesis of Impact and Process Research,* p. 15 (Washington, D.C.: U.S. Government Printing Office, 1975).

11. *Program Solicitation: Applied Research on the Benefits and Costs of Public Regulation* (Washington, D.C.: NSF/RANN, 1976).

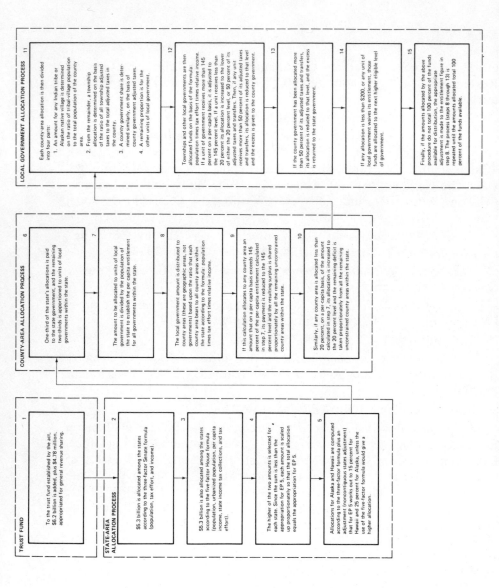

TRUST FUND

1

To the trust fund established by the act, $6.2 billion is added, plus $4.78 million, appropriated for general revenue sharing.

STATE-AREA ALLOCATION PROCESS

2

$5.3 billion is allocated among the states according to the three-factor Senate formula (population, tax effort, and income).

3

$5.3 billion is also allocated among the states according to the five-factor House formula (population, urbanized population, per capita income, state income tax collections, and tax effort).

4

The higher of the two amounts is selected for each state. Since the sum is less than the appropriation for EP 5, each amount is scaled up proportionately so that the total allocation equals the appropriation for EP 5.

5

Allocations for Alaska and Hawaii are computed according to the three-factor formula plus an adjustment (noncontiguous states adjustment) that for EP 5 works out to 15 percent for Hawaii and 25 percent for Alaska, unless the use of the five-factor formula would give a higher allocation.

COUNTY-AREA ALLOCATION PROCESS

6

One-third of the state's allocations is paid to the state government, and the remaining two-thirds is apportioned to units of local governments within the state.

7

The amount to be allocated to units of local government is divided by the population of the state to establish the per capita entitlement for all governments within the state.

8

The local government amount is distributed to county areas (these are geographic areas, not governments) based upon the ratio that each county area bears to all county areas within the state according to the formula population times tax effort times relative income.

9

If this calculation allocates to any county area an amount that on a per capita basis exceeds 145 percent of the county entitlement calculated in step 7, its payment is reduced to the 145 percent level and the resulting surplus is shared proportionately by all the remaining unconstrained county areas within the state.

10

Similarly, if any county area is allocated less than 20 percent, on a per capita basis, of the amount calculated in step 7, its allocation is increased to the 20 percent level and the remaining deficit is taken proportionately from all the remaining unconstrained county areas within the state.

LOCAL GOVERNMENT ALLOCATION PROCESS

11

Each county area allocation is then divided into four parts:
1. An amount for any Indian tribe or Alaskan native village is determined on the ratio of tribal-village population to the total population of the county area.
2. From the remainder, a township allocation is determined on the basis of the ratio of all township adjusted taxes to the total adjusted taxes in the county.
3. A county government share is determined similarly, on the basis of county government adjusted taxes.
4. A remaining proportion is for the other units of local government.

12

Townships and other local governments are then allocated funds on the basis of the formula population times tax effort times relative income. If a unit of government receives more than 145 percent on a per capita basis, it is adjusted to the 145 percent level. If a unit receives less than 20 percent its allocation is increased to the lower of either the 20 percent level, or 50 percent of its adjusted taxes and transfers. Then, if any unit receives more than 50 percent of its adjusted taxes and transfers, its allocation is reduced to that level and the excess is given to the county government.

13

If the county government has been allocated more than 50 percent of its adjusted taxes and transfers, its allocation is reduced to that level, and the excess is returned to the state government.

14

If any allocation is less than $200, or any unit of local government waives its entitlement, those funds are allocated to the next higher eligible level of government.

15

Finally, if the amounts allocated by the above procedure do not total 100 percent of the funds available for distribution, the appropriate adjustment is made to the entitlement figure in step 8. The process (steps 8 through 13) is repeated until the amounts allocated total 100 percent of the funds available.

Source: Reese Wilson et al., "General Revenue Sharing Formula Alternatives" (Menlo Park, Calif.: Stanford Research Institute, 1975), pp. 12–13.

Figure 6A–1. General Revenue Sharing Allocation Procedure for Entitlement Period 5.

Appendix 6A
How the Existing Formula
Works

The graphic illustration on the workings of the formula in figure 6A–1 was prepared by Stanford Research Institute for entitlement period five from information provided in Treasury publications.

Figure 6A–2, illustrating the workings of the formula, was prepared — most of the money goes to the biggest of the roughly 38,000 eligible jurisdictions. In effect, population drives the formula, but one jurisdiction with the same population as another will receive a large allocation if its per-capita income is lower or if its per-capita taxes are higher.

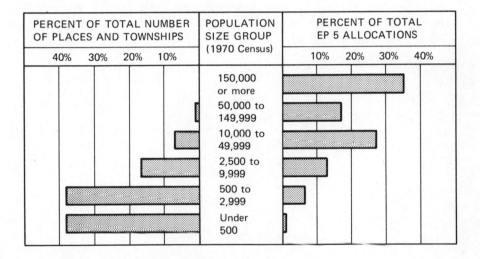

PERCENT OF TOTAL NUMBER OF PLACES AND TOWNSHIPS				POPULATION SIZE GROUP (1970 Census)	PERCENT OF TOTAL EP 5 ALLOCATIONS			
40%	30%	20%	10%		10%	20%	30%	40%
				150,000 or more				
				50,000 to 149,999				
				10,000 to 49,999				
				2,500 to 9,999				
				500 to 2,999				
				Under 500				

Source: *General Revenue Sharing Research Utilization Project, Volume II, Synthesis of Formula Research* (Washington, D.C.: U.S. Government Printing Office, 1975), p. 67.

Figure 6A–2. Places and Townships and Their Entitlement Period 5 Allocations by Population Size.

Proportion of revenues and expenditures acquired from GRS varies with type and size of government. In FY 1976 general revenue sharing entitlements are roughly 2.5 percent of anticipated state–local expenditures of $250 billion, but GRS is less than 2 percent of state government expenditures, 6.3 percent of county expenditures, 4.9 percent of municipal government expenditures, and 7.5 percent township expenditures.[1] In general, large, local government jurisdictions get more per capita than smaller ones because of their high tax effort. However, GRS as a percent of own taxes tends to be less in large places. Some limited function governments (Midwestern Townships) get up to one third of their revenues from GRS.

Note

1. *General Revenue Sharing Research Utilization Project, Volume II, Synthesis of Formula Research,* (Washington: U.S. Government Printing Office, 1975), pp. 8–9.

**Part II
Evaluation of Research**

7

Analytical Approach to Intergovernmental Aid Research

Paul R. Dommel

Since general revenue sharing (GRS) became a national policy in 1972, it has resulted in a growing and diverse body of political and economic research. With the proliferation of revenue sharing research, the immediately recognized problems are assimilating the multioutputs into a coherent analysis of revenue sharing and using the research findings as guides to policy maintenance or change. Less immediately perceived is the need to analyze GRS within the larger intergovernmental policy context it shares with other decentralizing allocation mechanisms that have emerged, principally the block grant. It is the purpose of this chapter to focus on the linkages that cut across both GRS and block grants to examine some general effects that the evolving, decentralizing intergovernmental aid process has on policy outcomes.

This chapter links three general policy study approaches: process, distributive–redistributive, and demand–supply analyses. The linkages, in turn, yield the following: (1) a tentative hypothesis requiring further research. Specifically, the intergovernmental aid system is linked to the politics of the national policy process in a way that is increasingly biasing the system toward distributive allocations. Both the process and the distributive allocation system restructure federal aid policy toward a demand-oriented policy. This tends to make it increasingly distributive in its impact; (2) a methodological approach by which the hypothesis can be tested; (3) a three-dimensional framework within which the growing of intergovernmental aid research can be analyzed to offer and validate other hypotheses

My appreciation to Sarah F. Liebschutz, research associate at The Brookings Institution, for her comments on a draft of this chapter.

The Frameworks

Process Analysis

Broadly stated, process analysis ranges from the making of an issue, through the process of policy formulation and adoption, to the impact of the policy as it is implemented.[a] Central to this process is the independent, but not readily quantified, variable politics that both shapes the issue, defines the substance, and structures the impact. A principal descriptive characteristic of the American policy process is that it is highly fragmented involving multiple role players with divergent goals, interacting and competing with each other to move and shape the policy in a particular direction. For significant national policy, this interplay is likely to involve the presidency, the bureaucracy, Congress, interest groups, and perhaps the invisible hand of a national interest. In the case of intergovernmental policy, this national configuration finds counterparts at the subnational levels as state and local political forces and decision processes further structure the policy and its impact. A principal consequence of this bargaining–compromise process is, as much policy literature asserts, policy incrementalism. That is, we take a problem, adopt a politically acceptable but limited approach to its solution, and then, step by step, we begin to push the margins of the policy outward, doing a bit more this year, perhaps a bit more the next. It is heralded as a process that provides both policy continuity and the satisfaction of a multiplicity of competing demands. By those less friendly toward the process, it is characterized as a system predominantly promoting political satisfaction rather than a process for basic problem solving.

Distributive–Redistributive Analysis

This type of analysis has become prominent in policy studies since the mid-1960s, developed basically from the conceptual framework of Theodore Lowi.[1] Distributive policies, Lowi said, are those that allocate benefits widely.[2] Such policies provide benefits, directly or indirectly, without regard to income levels of the recipients and include such policies as public works, environmental protection, public safety, and defense. Distributive policy could, therefore, be generally characterized as "something-for-everyone" even though the benefits may not be

---

[a] For illustrative examples of the sequential policy process, see James E. Anderson, *Public Policy-Making* (New York: Praeger Publishers, 1975); Charles O. Jones, *An Introduction to the Study of Public Policy* (Belmont, Calif.: Wadsworth Publishing Co., 1970); Charles E. Lindblom, *The Policy-Making Process* (Englewood Cliffs, N.J.: Prentice-Hall, 1968).

individually allocated or directly felt or perceived.[3] It is asserted here that distributive policies may also take the form of allocations to reflect unequal fiscal capacity among regions, states, and communities, and shift resources from richer *areas* to poorer areas. That is, distributive policies may have a fiscal equalization effect. While this would seem to contradict the principal characteristic of distributive policies as providing benefits without regard to income levels of recipients, the critical difference is between individuals or families as recipients and political jurisdictions as recipients. While equalization policies do differentiate among fiscal capacities of jurisdictional recipients and adjust allocations accordingly, they do, at the same time, provide some allocations or access to allocations to both rich and poor areas.

Redistributive policies, as defined by Lowi, are those involving resource allocations among social classes.[4] For analytical purposes, this definition is further refined for this chapter to mean those aimed at shifting resources either in the form of transfer payments or services, from higher income to lower income persons or families. Within this definition, a basic characteristic of redistributive policy in terms of such payments or services is that such policies structure in the principle of "nothing-for-some." That is, above established levels of income, individuals or families receive no benefits. This is seen in welfare, subsidized housing programs, and food stamp policies from which the ineligible middle and upper income groups derive no direct benefit.

Thus, in terms of policy impacts, redistributive policies focus on individuals and families and incorporate the principle of nothing-for-some, while distributive–equalization policies focus on jurisdictional or areal allocations and are heavily oriented toward something-for-all.

Supply–Demand Analysis

This chapter adopts the conceptual tools of the economists. The categorical-grant system providing federal aid for specific, narrowly defined purposes structures both the supply of and the demand for federal assistance.

The supply of federally assisted goods and services is most visibly shaped in the adoption of the policies themselves by specifying for what purposes funds will be provided. This federally sponsored structuring is, in turn, pushed downward to the state and local levels where only certain goods and services are funded with the federal money. The supply is further structured at subnational levels by the price effect of the categoricals.[5] That is, federal aid for certain programs has the effect of reducing the price of the aided programs at the state or local level. This further advantages the supply of the aided programs at the subnational levels by giving them a comparative price advantage in state and local budgeting processes through which required matching funds are provided. Thus, a federally aided program is likely to have more leverage among subnational decision makers than a program for which no federal aid is available.

The categorical system, as a structured supply policy, also has the effect of structuring demands at the subnational levels by giving comparative demand advantages to the bureaucratic and public beneficiaries of the aided programs while disadvantaging those outside of the aided programs in the competition for both national and subnational funds.

During the 1960s there was increasing dissatisfaction with the proliferating categorical-grant system because of red tape, program overlap, and the extensive national supervision involved. The categorical grants came to be seen by subnational officials as a complex bureaucratic tangle that gave federal decision makers too much discretionary authority and subnational policy makers too little. They were also seen as biasing the programs toward larger urban areas, concentrating a dispropor- tionately large share of the money in a relatively small number of cities. It was within this context of growing dissatisfaction with the categorical system that various proposals were advanced to simplify the system and reduce federal controls. The principal proposals included revenue sharing and block grants, representing a shift from supply to demand policy.

A demand policy is characterized here as one by which the national government provides funds to subnational units with few (block grants) or no conditions (revenue sharing) attached to their use. It is a demand policy in that it provides an "income" to subnational units to spend as they see fit (to oversimplify), with the actual expenditure decisions determined by competing demands at the subnational levels. Since the funds are unconditional or carry only broad nationally established conditions, it is a system of theoretically free demand competition with comparative advantages and disadvantages the result of subnational structures and processes *or* subnational processes institutionally modified by national policy. Stated another way, in supply policy the national structuring is attached to the specific uses of the funds while in demand policy use of the funds is made less conditional (or free of conditions) although the policy may have the effect of opening up demand competition through the restructuring of subnational decision-making processes. With the frameworks established, it would now be useful to restate the hypothesis within an expanded context.

During the 1970s there was a loss of confidence by some policy makers and the public at large in the ability of the national government to solve our complex social and economic problems. This loss of confidence, however induced or whether objective or subjective in origin, manifested itself in the form of new policies by which the national government provides financial support, an income, to subnational governments, but plays a significantly reduced role in specifying the uses of this income, that is, a shift from supply to demand policy. Accompanying this new direction of national policy is an emphasis on something-for-all rather than nothing-for-some allocation mechanisms—adoption of a more distributive intergovernmental allocation system. Recognizing that demand policy may advantage certain politically important groups at the subnational levels, national policy makers seek marginally to structure subnational decision making processes to open up state and local decision making to a wider range of competitive demands. In pursuing this goal, subnational policy outputs tend to be more distributive as the limited resources are earmarked for distributive purposes or become more politically distributed to give some satisfaction to the growing number of competing subnational demands.

Before proceeding, some further analytical points must be made.

This analysis is based on two obvious but important assumptions: (1) every community has physical and human needs that are not being met; (2) there are insufficient available public resources to meet all of these needs. Consequently, a major challenge to our political and policy processes is to structure allocation instruments to aid those communities with the greatest needs even if it means no allocations to those at the lowest end of the needs scale.

Another analytical point concerns the allocation mechanism itself. Allocation mechanisms contain two distinct elements: (1) *eligibility*—who may participate in the program, (2) *resource distribution*—the amount of funds those eligible will receive.[6] In distributive politics and policies, the emphasis tends to be on the eligibility component. In formulating intergovernmental aid policy, the operative political imperative is gaining sufficient political support for adoption and funding of the policy. Therefore, the initial problem is one of adopting sufficiently broad, politically optimum eligibility standards to insure majority support in the formulation and legitimation stages of the policy process.

The resource distribution component offers two principal allocation possibilities: (1) per-capita distributions, (2) distributions scaled to quantified measures of need. As shown in figure 7-1, the most distributive policy would be universal eligibility and per-capita distributions; a more redistributive outcome would be distributions scaled to need and limited eligibility based on need. While the typology would seem to imply mutually exclusive categories, distributive-redistributive allocations are better viewed as a continuum with many intermediate possibilities

ELIGIBILITY

		Universal	Limited
ALLOCATION	Per Capita	Distributive	Moderate Distributive
	Need	Moderate Redistributive	Redistributive

Source: Paul R. Dommel, "Urban Policy and Federal Aid: Redistributive Issues," *Urban Problems and Public Policy,* Robert L. Lineberry and Louis H. Masotti, eds., (Lexington, Mass.: Lexington Books, D.C. Heath Co. 1975) p. 161.

Figure 7-1. A Typology of Intergovernmental Assistance.

between the most distributive and most redistributive modes. It is now time to link the frameworks specifically to revenue sharing and block grants and explore the implications for the future of intergovernmental assistance policy.

General Revenue Sharing

The political history of general revenue sharing is illustrative of the linkages between process-distribution analysis and the emergence of demand-oriented intergovernmental aid policy.[b] It should be noted at the outset that in the formulation stage GRS had open to it, at least theoretically, the full range of distributive–redistributive allocation options. As a new program with new money, there were no established claimants to the funds and thus there was no problem of reallocation from one set of recipients to another. This set of conditions is not applicable to block grants that usually involve the consolidation of older programs and the politically sensitive task of reallocation.

From the time revenue sharing became a highly visible policy proposal in mid-1964 until its final passage in October 1972, the greatest difficulty faced by proponents of GRS was building and maintaining a coalition of support sufficient to gain adoption of the program. For the first four and a half years of that history, building that support was a slow

---

[b] For legislative histories of revenue sharing, see David A. Caputo and Richard L. Cole, *Urban Politics and Decentralization* (Lexington, Mass.: Lexington Books, D.C. Heath and Co., 1974) chaps. 1–3; Paul R. Dommel, *The Politics of Revenue Sharing* (Bloomington, Ind.: Indiana University Press, 1974); Richard P. Nathan et al., *Monitoring Revenue Sharing* (Washington: The Brookings Institution, 1975), pp. 344–72; Richard E. Thompson, *Revenue Sharing: A New Era in Federalism?* (Washington: Revenue Sharing Advisory Service, 1973).

process because it was clear that the concept was opposed by President Lydon B. Johnson. Without open and strong White House support, prospects for enactment were dim.

With the election of Richard M. Nixon in 1968, the prospects for revenue sharing immediately changed. With a presidential commitment to revenue sharing, the lobbying organizations began to unify their efforts to both shape the substance of the legislation and to put pressure on Congress for enactment. This coalition building resulted in a decision that determined which governmental units would be eligible to participate in the program. Very early in the Nixon administration the decision was made that nearly 39,000 units of general government would be eligible for GRS funds, a clearly distributive eligibility decision based on the belief that the unified support of mayors, city managers, county officials, governors, and state legislators would be necessary to force passage through a reluctant Congress. From that point on there was never any serious proposal or effort to reduce significantly the number of eligible participants. At the point when revenue sharing shifted from the politics of the impossible to the politics of the possible, it also became a something-for-everyone proposal.

This distributive approach was also found in formula allocation decisions. The original Nixon plan contemplated a distribution based principally on population with some adjustment for tax effort, a clearly distributive allocation approach. Congress consequently altered this to include an important need factor, per-capita income. In spite of Congress's substantial alteration of the distribution criteria, however, the end product tended to be oriented toward a distributive effect.

This is not to say that the formula resulted in no distributional differences among recipients. For example, on a per-capita basis, the initial ratio was approximately 2.5 to 1 between the 48 cities with over 300,000 population and the nearly 6,500 communities with fewer than 5,000 population.[7] The point to be noted, however, is that all of the nearly 18,500 municipalities received some funds. It should also be pointed out that the per-capita distributional advantage of the largest cities was nearly eliminated when the overlying state and county amounts were included for the municipalities. When calculated in this layered manner, the largest–smallest municipal ratio dropped to 1.16 to 1.0, indicating how much the municipal per-capita differences resulting from the formula allocation were diminished by the eligibility and allocations to 3,000 county units and the states.[8]

Another especially noteworthy distributive decision was the inclusion of a "floor" provision that had the effect of substantially increasing the entitlements of many small governmental units with limited functions, particularly midwest townships.[9]

In sum, the politics of policy formulation and the politics of policy legitimation resulted in a clearly distributive allocation policy for general revenue sharing. Within this distributive allocation politics of revenue sharing was distributive demand politics. Anticipating the need for broad support during the formulation of the policy, the Nixon administration, as noted, acceded to demands for participation by all units of general government. At the congressional level this demand politics took the form of adjustment and readjustment of formula alternatives to gain support from the largest number of law makers who themselves had shifted their early concern about the philosophy behind GRS to a more narrow interest of assuring that their constituencies got a share of the funds, that is, assuring that they received an income.

Distributive demand politics and outcomes was also linked to the "no strings" approach of revenue sharing. As noted earlier, categorical grants structure demand and supply both by specifying the purpose for which federal aid is available and by the price effect. Conversely, a no-strings approach greatly opens up this structured system. As the funds leave the national level as an income, there is no federally mandated set of preferred goods and services and thus, *theoretically,* at the subnational levels all demands for goods and services compete with equal probability of success and on the same price terms. Thus, the federally structured, supply-oriented policy of categorical grants becomes a more unstructured, subnational, demand-oriented policy under no strings revenue sharing.

The no-strings approach was an integral part of the original Heller–Pechman revenue sharing plan and was retained in the Nixon proposals in 1969 and 1971. In form, this no-strings approach was altered in the Congress (more specifically, the House Ways and Means Committee) by adoption of a system of priority categories for local governments. In substance, however, the priority category system was seriously eroded by another decision in the Ways and Means Committee to eliminate a local maintenance of effort provision. The net effect was to render the categories largely meaningless and make the system substantially no strings, allowing extensive local government substitution of their own funds with the GRS money. A Brookings Institution study stated that the substitution effect was more evident among older, larger, and more fiscally hard-pressed local governments. Wealthier, smaller, and less densely populated communities tended to use a higher proportion of their payments for new spending purposes.[10] The point emphasized here is that, while age and fiscal condition may be a determinant of actual substitution decisions, such decisions can be made with considerable ease by all recipients.

Previously the word "theoretically" was stressed in relation to free competition for funds at the subnational levels. The reports on state and local spending patterns underscore the theoretical nature of the competition. It must be emphasized that the aggregate data on expenditure patterns is based on the Actual Use Reports required by the law and it has become evident from the research that this data must be used with caution in interpreting the actual impact of general revenue sharing expenditures.[c] A University of Michigan study reported, ". . . the most that can be expected of ORS reports [Office of Revenue Sharing Actual Use Reports] is that they indicate the local accounts into which federal dollars were deposited; they do not (because they cannot) address the question of fiscal impact."[11] The Michigan study of five cities went on to say that, "once the continuance of revenue sharing receipts reaches a steady state, city governments are likely to use revenue increments according to priorities similar to the existing distribution of general fund expenditures."[12] The latter statement underscores the theoretical nature of the state and local open competition for funds.

As reported, the aggregate spending patterns indicated a state preference for educational expenditures (57 percent of GRS funds), in part to simplify the reporting procedures, while local governments showed a preference for public safety (36 percent), environmental protection (10 percent), and public transportation (19 percent).[13] The ORS reports showed that very low priority was given to the category of social services for the poor or aged (2 percent).[14] The expenditure reports for the first two years of the program suggested that the subnational governments tended to "spend" their funds for politically important, long-established, distributive programs.

This was not unexpected. During the congressional hearings spokesmen for policemen and firemen made it clear that they saw GRS funds as a new pool of resources from which they could demand pay increases.[15] Congress itself was not unaware of the potential pressure from public employee unions, tax rate pressures, and the considerable likelihood that the theoretical pure demand competition, particularly at the local levels, would become skewed toward certain expenditure areas. For this reason Congress sought to institutionalize a mechanism to open the competition for the untied money. This was part of the motivation behind the requirements, however ineffective, for publication in local newspapers of the planned and actual uses of the GRS money. In this way it was hoped that the funds would have higher public visibility and thus assist newer and less organized groups to gain access to the decision making process and thereby acquire a share of revenue sharing money.

The issue of a mechanism to foster citizen participation was raised by

---

[c] For a discussion of some of the problems of using the actual and planned use data, see Nathan et al., *Monitoring Revenue Sharing,* pp. 235–44.

Senator Russell Long, chairman of the Senate Finance Committee, during hearings on the House-passed version. Long's own preference was for a public referendum on local use of GRS money. This was strongly opposed by local officials and Long compromised on the newspaper advertisement provision.[16]

The result was a multilevel distributive-demand policy. At the national level, as a result of lobby pressures and congressional bread and butter politics, this took the form of a something-for-everyone policy in terms of both eligibility and distribution. At the local level, the distributive impact can be perceived (but not accurately measured) in the reported expenditure decisions that appear to be responses to demands from traditionally, politically important groups and interests.

One feedback message from this nationally instituted demand system was that subnational governments, particularly at the local level, have been more publicly responsive to the distributive demands of powerful groups than to the redistributive demands of the lower income groups.[17] One result was legislative efforts to restructure the system in a more supply-redistributive direction. An important example of this was the legislative proposal of Congressman Robert F. Drinan of Massachusetts.[18] Drinan, a member of the House Government Operations subcommittee with jurisdiction over revenue sharing and a liberal Democrat, voted for passage of revenue sharing in 1972.[d]

Among the principal changes sought by Drinan were application of the priority categories to state governments and the tightening of these categories at both the state and local levels by incorporating maintenance of effort provisions. The Drinan bill also required that a minimum percentage of GRS funds be spent in those categories benefiting low-income groups.[19] In effect, Drinan sought to introduce federally mandated requirements that would restructure the supply side of revenue sharing in a way that would advantage the lower income groups at the subnational levels and reduce the comparative demand advantages of certain long-established and politically important groups.

Drinan also contemplated opening up the demand side by introducing a requirement for public hearings in local decisions on the use of GRS money and establishment of a citizens' advisory committee.[20] The public hearings would represent something of a midway point between the newspaper advertisement provision of the 1972 law and the unsuccessful Long proposal for a public referendum.

It should be recognized that this approach seeks to restructure the

---

[d] A 1974 reorganization of House committees resulted in legislative jurisdiction over general revenue sharing being transferred from the House Ways and Means Committee to the Government Operations Committee.

supply and demand functions in favor of a particular group, in this case the lower income groups. The implicit assumption here is that the blame lies at the local level, that subnational officials cannot be trusted to make redistributive decisions with no strings money. It is not the purpose here to judge the validity of such an assessment. Rather, the significant point is the relationship at the national level between the coalition building process and the resultant distributive policy decisions and the consequences for policy, processes, and outcomes at subnational levels. Put another way, the distributive predisposition of state and local officials reflects the distributive orientation of the national policy and policy makers.

Block Grants

The block grant, like revenue sharing, was conceived as an allocation device that would decentralize intergovernmental policy to subnational levels. Unlike revenue sharing, however, the block grants have generally been consolidations of existing categorical-aid programs. The significance of the consolidation process is an implicit reallocation among recipients. The focus here is the community development block grant program (Title I of the Housing and Community Development Act of 1974, P.L. 93-383). This program was established by consolidation of seven urban-oriented categorical grants and authorized $2.5 billion for block grants the first year, increasing to $2.95 billion for fiscal years 1976 and 1977.

Two major points must be made:

1. As categorical programs, the seven consolidated aid programs had the characteristics of a supply policy; that is, they specified the types of projects to be aided, with the concomitant price and structured demand effects at subnational levels. The conversion of the project grants into a single consolidated block grant had the effect of shifting urban aid policy from a supply to a demand-oriented policy and perhaps (research is only getting underway on this program) is a distributive expenditure direction. The contention is that the policy process, combined with demand-oriented policy, will tend to yield more distributive outcomes.

2. Equally important to be noted is that the categorical grants were project grants, providing funds on the basis of an application from a particular community for a particular project. With the federal discretionary authority to approve or disapprove project grant applications, the project grant approach incorporated a nothing-for-some principle. This is not to say, however, that supply-oriented, nothing-for-some policy is thereby redistributive. Nothing-for-some can be quite distributive in both its allocation and its effect. For example, many expanding and reasonably

well-off metropolitan suburbs received water and sewer grants (one of the consolidated programs), a distributive allocation. Conversely, the model cities program was *relatively* more redistributive in the provision of a wide range of social services to lower income groups. It should also be noted that there was a form of distributive politics attached to the selection of some of the 147 model cities with key legislators in the program's policy process getting a project for their districts.

As noted, the categorical project grant was a nothing-for-some allocation system. Consequently, as the consolidation policy was formulated and the allocation issue was thus reopened, it was subject to demands for broader distributions. Basic in a shift from nothing-for-some to something-for-all policy is elimination or substantial reduction of bureaucratic discretionary authority to say who will receive the money. This is most readily achieved by shifting from a project grant to a formula grant approach under which a given amount of money is available annually for a given jurisdiction and that amount is based on quantified measures of need such as population, income, area, or some other need criteria. In the case of the community development program, the consolidation adopted a formula based on population, overcrowded housing, and poverty (weighted twice).

Earlier it was pointed out that a formula has two basic components — eligibility and resource distribution. In the case of the community development formula, the criteria had a redistributive bias. That bias, however, was significantly diminished by the eligibility component.[21]

The program adopted provided that 80 percent of the money, about $2.3 billion, be allocated to communities within metropolitan areas and 20 percent, about $550 million, for communities outside of metropolitan areas. This 80–20 division was the product of distributive politics and the need to gain the political support of nonurban law makers and organized interests. The 20 percent nonmetropolitan share resulted in a substantial increase in funds to these areas since they had received only about 12.8 percent under the categorical programs that were consolidated. (It should also be noted that the Senate sought to have the nonmetropolitan share set at 25 percent, thus reflecting the greater importance of the less urban states in that chamber.)[22]

Within the metropolitan areas, nearly 600 recipients were designated as *entitlement areas,* thereby assuring them of an annual, noncompetitive amount of money based on the formula. These entitlement areas included all metropolitan central cities, suburbs of 50,000 or more population, and urban counties that met certain population and community development requirements.

In addition to these nearly 600 metropolitan entitlement areas, smaller communities (less than 50,000) within metropolitan areas were made *eligible* for substantial discretionary funds These metropolitan discretionary funds will total about $830 million a year under the formula with distribution earmarked for communities with less than 50,000 residents.[e] This is a substantially improved position for these small metropolitan communities that received only about 11 percent of the urban categorical funds and had to compete for funds with the large cities. Under the consolidation, these same communities have about 40 percent of the money targeted for their use and they no longer compete with the larger jurisdictions.

Viewed overall, the new block grant program is considerably more distributive in its entitlements and eligibility than were some of the project grants that were consolidated. For example, only 147 selected communities were able to participate in model cities while the urban renewal program, by its nature, tended to be self-limiting. Combined, these two programs accounted for 90 percent of the urban categorical money. In total, only about 750 small (under 50,000) metropolitan and nonmetropolitan communities participated in the seven categorical urban grants during the period 1968–72. With the greater amount of funds, increased flexibility on their use, and more open-ended eligibility, it is likely that many more communities will be receiving block grant funds.

The central feature of the block grant approach is to reduce greatly federal restrictions on how the money can be spent. Block grants designate the general policy area for which the funds can be spent and establish some broad goals and thus are not as free of expenditure restrictions as general revenue sharing money. Nonetheless, the block grant does provide broad flexibility on use of the funds by local governments. The emphasis is on local planning and local discretionary authority. Further, the community development grant requires no matching local funds and thus the federal money does not have the local price effect that the categoricals had. Again, in supply–demand terms, the consequence was to shift the national supply policy and structured demands of the categoricals to a demand policy with a more unstructured demand system at the local level.

The shift from a supply to a demand policy was further evident in the requirements for local public hearings on how the money is spent. Again, with research just getting underway, it cannot be empirically stated what the consequences of this institutionalized public hearing process will be, but it is reasonable to hypothesize that the hearing process, combined with the greater flexibility on use of the money, will result in a broader

---

[e] This is the amount of metropolitan discretionary money that has been projected to be available in the sixth year of the program (fiscal year 1980) if the present program is extended beyond the initial three-year authorization.

range of local demands. The more distributive outcomes of block grants can take several forms—quick and highly visible projects; more geographical distribution of the projects around a community (something not easily achieved with model cities and urban renewal projects); reduced spending on model cities-initiated social service programs.

In short, local decisions will tend to be increasingly distributive, a policy outcome fostered by a distributive national allocation system, a nationally established mechanism (public hearings) to open up local decision making processes, and the dynamics of subnational politics.

Summary and Conclusions

The categorical system (supply policy), in specifying the uses of funds, has no inherently distributive or redistributive outcome. The distributive or redistributive result is a function of the specific national policy itself.

The current pattern of intergovernmental aid policy seems to be clearly oriented toward a demand policy. Under a long-term condition of scarce resources, a demand policy will affect the prospects for solving severe social and economic problems by distributing a larger portion of available resources to meet a wider range of demands.

Revenue sharing and block grants (demand policy) are likely to have more distributive outcomes. This is the probable consequence of two factors: (1) the tendency of national policy makers to adopt distributive allocation mechanisms, and (2) the nature of the subnational demand processes that national policy seeks to structure toward more free demand competition.

At the national level, this distributive outcome is fostered by a policy process that deals first with the eligibility component of the allocation mechanism and then the resource distribution element. The demands of distributive politics result in broad eligibility with some subsequent scaling of allocations through a needs formula. The result tends toward a something-for-all allocation system.

If this sequence of decisions were reversed, a different outcome is possible. If consideration is first given to definition of need, followed by eligibility standards, a more redistributive outcome is possible. This can be achieved by making eligible only those jurisdictions whose needs meet an established threshold. That is, apply the nothing-for-some needs test approach of welfare and welfare services policy to intergovernmental aid systems. Given the politics of federal aid distribution decisions, the reversed sequence is not likely to be adopted. The point here is not whether it can or cannot be or should or should not be; rather, that the national policy and decision process itself is a significant variable that tends to produce certain outcomes.

At the subnational level, the structure and the political weight of demands are a major determinant of outcomes. It is assumed by some that national policy to open up the subnational decision-making processes will result in more redistributive decisions. Perhaps, but a more open demand system may also result in more distributive decisions in order to give some satisfaction to the wider range of demands, many of which are for distributive purposes.

It is at this point where this chapter departs from its own hypothesis and hopefully is suggestive of a vertical and horizontal process-outcome framework within which a wide range of emerging intergovernmental aid research can be applied and interrelated.

Notes

1. Theodore J. Lowi, "American Business, Public Policy, Case Studies, and Political Theory," *World Politics,* vol. 16 (July 1964), pp. 677–715.

2. Ibid., p. 690.

3. Paul R. Dommel, "Urban Policy and Federal Aid: Redistributive Issues," *Urban Problems and Public Policy,* Robert L. Lineberry and Louis H. Masotti, eds. (Lexington, Mass.: Lexington Books, D.C. Heath and Co., 1975) pp. 159–61.

4. Lowi, "American Business, Public Policy," p. 691.

5. Murray L. Weidenbaum, *Potential Impacts of Revenue Sharing,* Reprint No. 26 (Washington: American Enterprise Institute, October 1974), p. 4.

6. Dommel, "Urban Policy and Federal Aid," pp. 160–61.

7. Richard P. Nathan et al., *Monitoring Revenue Sharing,* (Washington: The Brookings Institution, 1975), table 5–10, pp. 130–31.

8. Ibid.

9. Ibid., pp. 160–62.

10. Ibid, p. 230.

11. Thomas J. Anton et al., "Understanding the Fiscal Impact of General Revenue Sharing," *General Revenue Sharing:* Research Utilization Project, vol. 2, *Summaries of Impact and Process Research* (Washington: National Science Foundation, September, 1975), p. 31.

12. Ibid., pp. 31–32.

13. U.S., Department of the Treasury, Office of Revenue Sharing, *Second Annual Report of the Office of Revenue Sharing,* March 1, 1975, table p. 16.

14. Ibid.

15. Paul R. Dommel, *The Politics of Revenue Sharing,* (Bloomington, Ind.: Indiana University Press, 1974), pp. 135–36.

16. Richard E. Thompson, *Revenue Sharing: A New Era in Federalism?* (Washington: Revenue Sharing Advisory Service, 1973), pp. 110–11.

17. See remarks of Congressman Robert F. Drinan, *Congressional Record,* vol. 121, no. 103, June 26, 1975 (Daily Edition), pp. H6274–78.

18. H.R. 8329, 94th Cong., 1st sess., June 26, 1975.

19. Drinan bill, H.R. 8329, Sec. 103.

20. Ibid., Sec. 121(a) (2) and (3).

21. Dommel, "Urban Policy and Federal Aid," pp. 168–71.

22. U.S., Senate, Committee on Banking, Housing and Urban Affairs, *Report: Housing and Community Development Act of 1974,* Cmte Rpt. 93-693, 93rd Cong., 2nd sess., Feb. 27, 1974, p. 15.

8

Policy Analysis and Political Action: Advice to Princelings

Donald B. Rosenthal

Most students of public policy have come to view rationalistic models[a] of policy formulation and policy implementation with considerable skepticism. Such skepticism grows out of recognition that political reality does not proceed in the neat fashion postulated by the model builders. While it may be argued that we cannot rely upon rationalistic models for establishing and sustaining an appropriate relationship between policy analysis and advice, on the one hand, and political action, on the other, it is questionable whether intellectual alternatives like incrementalism or "muddling through" are adequate as alternative guides to policy actions.[1] Except for that school of thinking convinced that to do nothing or very little in many instances is superior policy advice to any other course of action available,[b] it becomes difficult to develop an intellectually defensible strategy for research and advice about the policy process that promises to yield clear and concise recommendations that decision makers will find useful.

Further, one can argue, as Daniel P. Moynihan has, that the role of social scientist should not be conceived as including a contribution to policy formulation. (What the social scientist does *as citizen* is quite another matter.) There is a danger, he suggests, that intellectuals drawn into the policy process will tend to confuse theories with data-based research, thus producing advice with the patina of legitimacy provided by academic or institutional research affiliations but without the modesty to

---

[a] I have in mind such items as Yehezkel Dror, *Public Policy Re-Examined* (San Francisco: Chandler, 1968); and Harold D. Lasswell and Daniel Lerner, *The Policy Sciences* (Palo Alto: Stanford University Press, 1951). To some extent, the label also applies to works like Mancur Olson, *The Logic of Collective Action* (Cambridge, Mass.: Harvard University Press, 1965).

[b] The great proponent of that perspective is, of course, Edward C. Banfield in his *The Unheavenly City* (Boston: Little, Brown, 1970) but the perspective is perhaps best summarized in the phrase "benign neglect" attributed to Daniel P. Moynihan. A good argument against allowing current processes to work themselves out "naturally" may be found in Anthony Downs in his *Urban Problems and Prospects* (Chicago: Markham, 1970), esp. pp. 37–45.

145

recognize the weak intellectual basis upon which that advice may be grounded. Moynihan points to the "dual" nature of the American social scientist as both a "seeker after truth," and as a person who "is also very likely to be a passionate partisan of social justice and social change."[2] He suggests that this passion can be controlled only if the social scientist adopts the maxim that "the role of social science lies not in the formulation of social policy, but in the measurement of its results."[3] Thus, the social scientist's job is to perfect the collection and analysis of social data rather than to be the propagator or publicist of policy alternatives. That task, presumably, is to be left to the politician.[c]

Moynihan's formulation of the problem can be treated in various ways, some of them perhaps not intended by him. For example, he leaves open the possibility that researchers can readily assume the role of political eunuchs when, in reality, they are likely to be drawn into the political process by their very activity, sometimes in spite of themselves. This is particularly the case where recommendations for change flow from analysis of experiences with existing policy—a much more common phenomenon than the innovative situation described by Moynihan in his study of the origins of the poverty program. (Even there the failure of past program efforts was an important factor in generating the search for alternatives.) It requires much more forebearance than most human beings are likely to have to expect social scientists to study the consequences of a policy but to stop short of making recommendations grounded on the findings that flow from such research.

The realities of public policy research are also complicated by at least two other factors. First, sponsored research increasingly carries expectations by sponsors that such research will be "applied" to substantive policy recommendations. Thus, the role of policy adviser is sometimes forced on the researcher by a funding agency or by the expected "users" of research findings. (These "users" include legislative committees, agencies within the bureaucracy, government interest groups[d] and various citizen organizations.) Pressure mounts on the researcher to produce policy recommendations even where the data may be open to question. The greatest danger in such a situation, of course, is that the intellectual may be so drawn into the political process that important

---

[c] Especially relevant to this chapter is Moynihan's response to his critics on this point in his "Introduction to the Paperback Edition," *Maximum Feasible Misunderstanding* (New York: The Free Press, 1969), pp. xxix–xxxiii. While he attributes considerable utility to social science, he is strongly opposed to the notion that those with social science expertise have any special claim "to prescribe what is good for other people" (p. xxx).

[d] These groups are examined by Donald H. Haider in his *When Governments Come to Washington* (New York: Free Press, 1974).

alternatives in the form either of experiential data or policy recommendations will be excluded from consideration in order to please the sponsor. (This is a problem to which Moynihan aptly points with respect to foreign policy advisers drawn from universities and "think tanks" in connection with the Vietnam War.)

A second consideration facing some researchers who wish to remain aloof from roles as policy advisers is that they may be confronted by what I will identify as *advocacy research* produced by many of the groups mentioned above as "users" of academic research as well as by other professional organizations associated with a particular policy arena. While research produced by such groups may not always proceed on the basis of the highest canons of social science, in the marketplace of ideas and, even more important, among actors in the political process unfamiliar with methodological niceties, the status of findings from such research may be treated on a par equal to the findings from a study produced by the most dispassionate of observers. The political reality, therefore, may be that the latter will find themselves vying for attention for their studies with advocacy researchers; their sponsoring agencies (even if they are relatively nonprogrammatic bodies like the National Science Foundation) may feel some impulse to serve their own organizational needs by encouraging the production of "practical" policy results that can be presented to congressional committees; and the researcher will be forced into a role in the political arena.

The Case of General Revenue Sharing

The discussion thus far has been a prelude to consideration of the relationships among policy analysis, policy advice, and political action in respect to general revenue sharing (GRS). GRS is an interesting case in point for examining the kinds of issues alluded to earlier because it emerged, at least in part, out of the thinking of two academic economists closely tied to the federal policy network, Walter Heller and Joseph Pechman, and was influenced in the course of formulation and implementation by other policy analysts.

Nevertheless, GRS is not a policy quite in the Moynihan tradition. Following the lead provided by Moynihan in his study of the War on Poverty, a literature has developed that appears to be dedicated to the study of why programs do not work or, if they do (by some miracle) manage to work, why they work in ways that may not have been intended by their legislative advocates or by actors who participate in implementation of the policy.[e] Such studies demonstrate a variety of attitudes toward the policy process and toward political life, in general. These range from rationalistic treatments of the policy process that regard politicians as policy cowards reluctant to take strong political stands by clearly enunciating programmatic goals and developing effective instruments of policy action to carry out those goals to those studies that deal with politicians and bureaucrats as men and women caught in organizational webs whose imperatives they cannot escape. Between these extremes of free will and determinism lies a zone of political pragmatism where many political actors are seen to operate.

The conclusion of many of these studies is that the defects as well as the merits of policy making and policy implementation in the United States derive from the way in which the intergovernmental system is structured.[f] Short of advocating a thoroughgoing reform or revolution in the American political system, it is unclear which policy recommendations usefully may be seen to flow from such accumulated wisdom.[g] Nevertheless, a decade of experience with research on programs that have gone awry has not apparently sated the federal government and other funding organizations, which continue to sponsor research intended to yield policy recommendations. Although there is perhaps less faith than there was in the halcyon days of PPBS and cost-benefit analysis that the application of social science techniques to problems of public policy will relieve actors of the necessity of political choice, there is still faith both on the part of researchers and such funding organizations as the National Science Foundation (NSF) that policy evaluation can make a contribution to the political process not only in terms of analyzing why programs have

---

[e] In addition to the study by Moynihan, these include such studies as Jeffrey Pressman and Aaron Wildavsky, *Implementation* (Berkeley and Los Angeles: University of California Press, 1973); Martha Derthick, *New Towns In-Town* (Washington, D.C.: The Urban Institute, 1972); and Bernard J. Frieden and Marshall Kaplan, *The Politics of Neglect* (Cambridge, Mass. and London, Eng.: MIT Press, 1975). Also see many of the items that have appeared in *The Public Interest* reviewing policy failures, for example, David A. Musto, "Whatever Happened to 'Community Mental Health'?," *The Public Interest*, #39 (Spring 1975), 53–79.

[f] Strong expression of support for the existing intergovernmental system may be found in the works of Daniel J. Elazar including his *American Federalism: A View from the States*, 2nd ed. (New York: Thomas Y. Crowell, 1972). With respect to revenue sharing, see his "Amending the Revenue Sharing Act to Encourage Local Government Modernization," in General Accounting Office, *Revenue Sharing and Local Government Modernization: A Conference Report*, Washington, D.C., April 1975, pp. 48–88. Skepticism about the system may be found in Samuel H. Beer, "The Modernization of American Federalism," *Publius*, 3 (Fall 1973), 49–95; and Michael D. Reagan, *The New Federalism* (New York: Oxford University Press, 1972).

[g] In that regard, see James L. Sundquist and David W. Davis, *Making Federalism Work* (Washington, D.C.: Brookings, 1969). Also see the various contributions (other than Elazar's) to General Accounting Office, *Revenue Sharing*.

gone wrong but as a basis for suggesting changes in programs that may be operating according to expectations.

In fact, contrary to many previous experiences, GRS is one such "successful" program. Perhaps its very "success" has been responsible for producing the minor research industry that has grown up around the study of the program. There are a number of peculiar features of GRS as a national program, some of which are examined below, but there is no question that it has spawned considerable research that has made use of a variety of methodologies to study the performance of the program. Included in this body of research are an especially large number of pieces of what I have labelled advocacy research. Such research as well as the somewhat more dispassionate variety sponsored by bodies like NSF and Brookings has formed a substantial backdrop against which future decisions about alterations in the program (or its outright abolition) may take place. In the process, researchers have become part of the political process, for the availability of their research findings is a free political good that need not have an advocate researcher tied to it. Rather, the findings may be used by persons charged with political or administrative responsibilities or "users" to bolster their own political opinions or their own standing in the political process.

In this chapter I review some of the literature devoted to the study of GRS. These studies include histories and critiques of the policy formulation process, formula studies, expenditure analyses, opinion surveys.

Policy Formulation Studies

Studies of policy formulation are perhaps among the most established areas of policy research. Two types of studies are discussed in this section, those we may identify as *legislative histories* and others that may be regarded as *program critiques*. Unlike program evaluations, which are produced after a program has gone into effect and its consequences can be examined, program critiques are part of the original body of analytical materials surrounding the formulation of a program. One measure of the true success of a program may be the extent to which such critiques disappear or are reduced in scope from broad-ranging opposition to opposition based on particular features of the program.

Legislative histories are an area in which social scientists (especially political scientists) feel peculiarly at home.[h] Yet, aside from demonstrat-

---

[h] For legislative histories, see David A. Caputo and Richard L. Cole, *Urban Politics and Decentralization* (Lexington, Mass.: Lexington Books, D.C. Heath, 1974), pp. 17–65; Paul R.

ing how the motives of various actors were orchestrated into a set of policy declarations that may or may not have yielded specific directions to government actors, it is not clear what policy consequences may flow from such studies. It is true that the study of program goals can yield researchable questions for others to pursue, but there is no inherent logical sense in which policy actions can or should flow from findings that result from legislative case studies. At the most, perhaps, one can contend that such histories alert us to the boundaries of the politically possible and force us to take those parameters into account in putting forward recommendations for change that will be politically acceptable. Even such a modest proposition requires at least two caveats. First, the boundaries of political acceptability change over time, so that self-limitation may be both less necessary and less wise than it may appear at first. Second, policy suggestions bolstered by political experience may themselves generate political discussion that alters the way in which the politically acceptable is defined.

In any case, legislative histories of GRS show that at least three major goals were to be found among the motives of those supporting the program:

1. To make federal resources available with few strings to state and local governments
2. To encourage those governments to implement their preferences for expenditures without close supervision by federal actors
3. To strengthen generalist officials (both elected and appointed) at both state and local levels vis-à-vis program specialists, thereby reversing the process of policy fragmentation previously encouraged by the multiplication of categorical grants.

As we shall see in the following sections, studies have been concerned with each of these goals and, by most standards, the program should be judged a success insofar as it has managed to achieve any or all of these goals, although the evidence is not yet strong on the third goal.

Even if the program's goals have been achieved in a narrow sense, there are many critics who were dissatisfied with its original intentions and whose analyses of the program continue to reflect basic reservations about the principles the program sought to realize. Such critics come in many shapes and sizes. First are those who accept what the program was

Dommel, *The Politics of Revenue Sharing* (Bloomington: Indiana University Press, 1974); Haider, *When Governments Come to Washington,* pp. 257–82; Richard P. Nathan, Allen D. Manvel, and Susannah E. Calkins, *Monitoring Revenue Sharing* (Washington, D.C.: Brookings, 1975), esp. pp. 13–33 and 344–72; and Richard E. Thompson, *Revenue Sharing: A New Era in Federalism?* (Washington, D.C.: The Revenue Sharing Advisory Service, 1973).

intended to be but wish for additional "strings." These strings might have included stronger requirements on local governments to manage themselves better through reforms in budgetary procedures, development of greater managerial capacity, or forms of increased intergovernmental cooperation.[i] A second "string" would have required stronger evidence than is presently the case of citizen participation and provided a mechanism for punishing noncompliance; a third would have done the same for discriminatory behavior.

If such critics still basically support the GRS program, others have been more skeptical of the ideology of "new federalism" under which it was launched. Thus, critics like Michael Reagan and Lawrence Susskind have expressed a strong distrust of state and local governments presumably based on their observation of the operation of other intergovernmental programs.[4] They wish to maintain, if not actually to enhance, strong central direction in the operation of the federal system. The unhappiness of these analysts and others with past experiences of categorical program operation under the Kennedy and Johnson administration does not persuade them of the wisdom of allocating "free money" under GRS to states and localities unless those governments are required to demonstrate an adequate commitment to national (presumably more "liberal") values.

In these concerns, they are joined by a number of "cosmopolitan" public interest organizations some of whom have conducted their own research. Typified by the National Clearinghouse on Revenue Sharing, which set about the task of monitoring revenue sharing with the cooperation of groups like the Urban Coalition and the League of Women Voters, these groups have produced an impressive (albeit uneven) quantity of case materials.[j] In this case, as in so many others, the conflicting political values present at the creation of the program led to programs of research that reflected strongly held values. This raises an important issue to which we will return again later: Is "disinterested" research necessarily better than "committed" research? To anticipate that later discussion, we should note that the question as stated here may be misleading if not actually a product of false dichotomization.

---

[i] For an important congressional perspective on the need for local government reform, see Henry S. Reuss, *Revenue Sharing: Crutch or Catalyst for State and Local Governments?* (New York: Praeger, 1970). Also see, General Accounting Office, *Revenue Sharing.*

[j] Useful summary items include Patricia W. Blair, "General Revenue Sharing in American Cities: First Impressions," Washington, D.C.: National Clearinghouse on Revenue Sharing, December 1974; American Friends Service Committee, "Revenue Sharing in the South: A New Tool of Discrimination," Philadelphia, July 1974; and Carol M. Rose, "Citizen Participation in Revenue Sharing: A Report from the South," Southern Regional Council, Southern Governmental Monitoring Project, October 1975.

In any event, one of the interesting aspects of GRS is that it generated policy research at a very early stage inspired by groups deeply committed to the values of "creative federalism," whereas those who supported the program saw it as an effective means of allowing state and local government an area of discretion in making choices suitable to their own needs. Both ideological positions yielded programs of research, although the character of the critical research has been either to emphasize specific shortcomings of the program (in the monitoring materials) or to seek fairly substantial changes. Research reflecting satisfaction with the program is less explicitly stated as such but appears as a hidden assumption of much of the empirical material that bolsters the status of GRS by pointing to its popularity among state and local officials, among the general public or among Congressmen.

Aside from those critics of "new federalism," who perceived fundamental defects in the program itself, recommendations that have flowed from GRS research rarely go to questions of political system change. More commonly, such program critiques are concerned with specific features of the form the program took. Some of the findings of such research may be disquieting to observers but, as we shall see, there is enough mixed evidence on many items to leave matters open for policy actors to proceed undeterred by the threat of public wrath. Indeed, evidence is so mixed that political actors have been left with considerable freedom either to proceed in reforming the program along the lines suggested by critics or to leave the program much as it is.

The Formula Studies[k]

A crucial part of the legislative process with respect to GRS involved the specification of terms on which federal resources were to be distributed to state and local governments. Once formulas were constructed and implemented through the collection and application of socioeconomic data a large part of the program was in place in a way unusual among contemporary federal programs. The Office of Revenue Sharing (ORS) was also designed to see its own operations largely in terms of handing out money with a minimal amount of oversight. Thus, the normally pivotal role of the federal bureaucracy in turning a legislative program into

---

[k] In addition to Nathan, Manvel, and Calkins, *Monitoring Revenue Sharing,* see the various contributions to National Science Foundation, Research Applied to National Needs, *General Revenue Sharing: Research Utilization Project,* vol. 1: *Summaries of Formula Research,* July 1975. [Hereafter, studies in the series of research reports sponsored by NSF will be referred to by short title indicating in which volume of the recent summary series descriptions of the studies may be found. For the longer unpublished reports, NSF-RANN and the authors are the sources.]

implemented policy was not of great moment in the case of GRS. This closed off one area of policy research but made another unusually important: the manner in which allocations were made to states and localities and the consequences of the formula for those localities.

Thus, the complex formula alternatives adopted by Congress for allocating each dollar of available funds has provided a rich research field for exploration by economists, in particular, and for others of a technical bent. On the basis of manipulation of various factors built into the formula, a number of recommendations for change have been made. Among the more widely discussed are: alteration in the existing 145 percent ceiling; abolition of the 20 percent floor; change in the weight given to various factors on which the formula is constructed; and reconsideration of the distributive rules that uniformly allocate funds to the states and their respective local governments in one-third to two-thirds shares and among localities in ways that do not presently take into account variations among local governments in administrative responsibilities.

On their own terms, some of the exercises in formula manipulation are among the best models of policy research leading to political advice. They usually proceed from a clear set of assumptions about the factors being changed and examine the consequence of such changes. Even where such studies assume a posture of advocacy, at their best they harness and present their data and the methods used to analyse that data in a systematic fashion that is likely to be accessible to readers trained in data analysis.[1] The latter can then separate the author's biases from those data. (For less well-educated readers, however, the organization and presentation of the data may be obscure and reliance on the recommendations that flow from the findings may be highly dependent on the trust one places in the researcher.[m])

Given the narrowness of concerns of research of this character, however, there are three problems that need to be mentioned in connection with making formula research truly useful for policy action. First, and most important, very few pieces of formula research are capable of making the leap from political units to public benefits. By this I mean that discussions of formulas essentially are dealing with the way in which

---

[1] A particularly interesting example of this is Robert P. Strauss and Peter Harkins, *The 1970 Undercount and Revenue Sharing* (Washington, D.C.: The Joint Center for Political Studies, 1974); also see G. Ross Stephens, "State Responsibility for Public Services and General Revenue Sharing," NSF-RANN, vol. 1.

[m] The emphasis of this argument should not be taken to imply that formula research and the recommendations that flow from it are all that simple a process to conduct even for highly skilled data analysts. In fact, disagreements about the adequacy of various kinds of data and the appropriate interpretations to be made of the relationships between data and the social situations they are intended to represent can become quite problematic.

GRS funds are distributed to selected units of government. Alterations in the formula may favor some units over others but it is by no means clear that target groups within populations subsumed under a governmental unit will be favored as a result. Thus, to advocate removing the 145 percent ceiling need not lead, as some advocates of such a change seem to assume, to greater expenditures on benefits for the poor and the socially deprived *unless* the recipient governments choose to apply their funds in such a way. In principle, one could compare localities operating under such a ceiling to less handicapped communities to see what some of the behavioral consequences would be, but thus far I am not aware of any studies that present data in such a way as to combine formula concerns and behavioral analysis in a mode that serves this purpose.[n]

Second, most formula research tends to accept the program principles of GRS. As a result, there is little effort to venture into the thorny problems of trade-offs between GRS and various categorical grants in delivering resources to localities. Since little formula research seems to be tied directly to the study of budgetary decision making or local expenditure patterns, the policy consequences of formula research are often left hanging on the question of alternative policy instruments and even on the issue of the empirical effectiveness of GRS as a policy instrument in its own right.[o]

The two previous points lead to a third: there is little sense of political possibilities among formula researchers. The latter are largely economists, operating within a fairly airless closed universe of assumptions and data generation. The point may be slightly overstated, perhaps, because some formula research is conducted by persons who in fact have been actively engaged in policy advice in the past. Nevertheless, there is a surprising political naivete reflected in some of these proposals. At the same time, the value biases of formula researchers are fairly prominent in their *choice* of factors to study. Why otherwise do they regard certain distributive features of the formula as problematic? It may be all very well to tell a politician that he or she should abandon the 145 percent limitation but it would be better if the politician could be persuaded that the political consequences of such a change were not destructive of other values he might hold. Here the policy analyst is likely to be at a loss with the result that a gap between policy analysis (and advice) and policy action becomes more evident than when the formula researcher is left to his own more limited devices. Thus, in a peculiar fashion there may be a political safety

---

[n] Presumably such a capability is built into the Nathan study but I have not yet seen the second volume of that series.

[o] One of the more interesting efforts to deal with this problem may be found in Catherine H. Lovell et al., "The Effects of General Revenue Sharing on Ninety-Seven Cities in Southern California," NSF-RANN, vol. 2.

valve built into formula research that maintains some of the integrity of the distinct roles of policy analyst and political actor by casting the role of formula researcher in fairly circumscribed routines.

Expenditure Research[p]

If formula research is often respectable social science, there is a good deal of debate about the appropriate standing of research on patterns of expenditure. Here we get into what may be called "the great fungibility farrago." Among formula researchers there may be some disagreement about the quality of data and the appropriateness of particular data for measuring a given social attribute but there does not appear to be quite the same level of heated exchange involved as in the case of those who have been involved in expenditure research. Part of this conflict arises from a concern with research methods; another part from the way in which findings are understood.

With respect to research methods, there is considerable disagreement among researchers over the reliability of data generated from various sources. Thus, the Planned and Actual Use Reports have come in for a good deal of condemnation as tools of research, even though critics and supporters of GRS alike make use of those data to buoy their policy arguments. Even if it is agreed that respondents to ORS's inquiries or to the questionnaires circulated by other researchers try to respond to the questions posed to them in all honesty (and some doubt has been raised about respondent motivation), it is not clear that most localities' spokesmen are capable of answering those inquiries. Given the complexity of budgetary procedures in some communities, the timing of GRS vis-à-vis regular budgetary processes, considerations of the "meaning" of particular expenditures (how, for example, they properly should be assigned to the different ORS expenditure categories), not to mention the complications introduced into budgetary routines by tax reductions that resulted from the arrival of GRS, expenditure patterns may often be a matter of local guesswork.

It has been argued that one of the ways required to get around the methodological problem is closer field observation. Studies employing field research have attempted to do this and may have come closer to establishing the truth of expenditure patterns.[q] Yet, at the end of the

---

[p] In addition to the studies by Caputo and Cole, Lovell, and Nathan, see Thomas J. Anton et al., "Understanding the Fiscal Impact of General Revenue Sharing," NSF-RANN, vol. 2.

[q] On this, see the studies by Anton and Lovell. The problem apparently does not arise at the state level where Wright and Kovenock find a strong relationship between published state expenditure data and actual expenditures. See Deil S. Wright and David Kovenock,

elaborate research process, policy recommendations that may fruitfully be advanced as a result of better expenditure data are limited in scope. Indeed, in spite of the fungibility controversy, the ORS expenditure categories are probably morally neutral; too often observers have tended to invest them with value commitments of their own. Thus, for some of the monitoring organizations the clear evidence (from whatever source it is gathered) that only a tiny proportion of GRS funds goes for social services for the poor and aged or for other expenditures that are demonstrably and directly beneficial to such groups raises very serious questions about the desirability of the GRS program.

The result of much research into expenditures, therefore, is of little policy relevance short of program abolition or severe recategorization, perhaps with closer specification of federal purposes. Reporting the data, as in so many cases of social science, says nothing in itself. The policy researcher thus must either become a major intervening factor in the reporting of results or what he or she has to report is left to the confused political interpretations of others.

To further complicate the matter, we do not at present appear to have a satisfactory set of measurers of actual expenditures that will allow us really to determine how much of GRS goes into direct benefits for the poor and the aged as opposed to benefits for social agencies that in their name expend large sums on their own operations; at the same time, we know little or nothing about the social benefits of some of the expenditures on "hardware" to which critics have objected. High expenditures on public safety, transportation, and recreation need not be "bad," as some critics seem to assume when they condemn the contrast between such expenditures and monies spent on health or social services, until we know more definitely than we do now that an equitable proportion of benefits is not going to persons that deserve a share in those "hard" services.[r]

Given the uncertainty of the debate over expenditures, recommendations for action by critics of GRS are given free rein. These range from abolition of GRS through greater specification of expenditure categories (moving the program much closer, as a result, to some form of block grant) to greater assurance that program benefits will be distributed in a nondiscriminatory fashion with significant citizen participation. The cacophony of assumptions and the diversity of recommendations that flow from research findings about expenditure patterns make it doubtful

---

"Assessing the Impact of General Revenue Sharing in the Fifty States: An Analysis Based on Participants' Perspectives," NSF-RANN, vol. 2.

[r] Save for some graduate student papers produced in a seminar conducted at the University of Michigan by Thomas Anton, very little effort has been made to identify the way in which benefits from GRS are allocated to various segments of the local population.

that political actors can be expected to make substantial use of the results of such research except to support positions they already hold. Under the circumstances, that is both a political gain and a setback for policy research since it reveals how slender may be the distinctions that separate "respectable" social science from less well-grounded advocacy research.

Opinion Surveys [s]

There are two species of opinion research: surveys of citizens (both the well informed and the less informed) and surveys of political actors. Characteristic of the first are a few studies that measure citizen knowledge, support, and satisfaction with respect to GRS. The findings are generally favorable to GRS but knowledge among the general public is so limited and even among the knowledgeable the intensity of support so thin that one comes away from such reports with a feeling that the program could be abolished or radically altered without causing much public controversy or much opposition among citizens. However, such a reading of the data is my personal view since what citizen survey data is available has generally been framed in a supportive direction without consideration of more complex issues like the trade-offs citizens might be willing to make in connection with other policy alternatives.

On a more sophisticated level are those studies that have examined the reactions of public officials to the operations of GRS. Again, support is widespread, but the intensity of such support is hard to estimate. Operating under inflationary pressures, confronted with federal categorical grant impoundments (particularly during the Nixon administration), and faced with revenue declines associated with narrow resource bases in a recession and allegedly regressive tax systems that make their situations even more difficult, local and state officials unsurprisingly respond in favor of GRS.

The policy recommendations that flow from such findings are peculiarly uninteresting. Only rarely do such studies examine the political correlates of opinion of program impacts in such areas as gains in power by governmental generalists as opposed to program specialists, the effects of the program on elected as opposed to administrative officials, and the

---

[s] For one important public survey, see Frederic M. Mason and Rees Toothman, "The General Public and Community Leaders View the General Revenue Sharing Program," NSF-RANN, vol. 2. For the perspectives of state and local officials, see F. Thomas Juster, "A Survey of the Impact of General Revenue Sharing"; and Steven A. Waldhorn, "Planning and Participation: General Revenue Sharing in Ten Large Cities," both in NSF-RANN, vol. 2. Also see the study done by Wright and Koveneck and my annotated bibliography included as "The Impact of General Revenue Sharing in State and Local Government" in the same volume.

relative advantages or disadvantages to governments operating under categorical grants as opposed to GRS. In sum, the opinion data may be tied only loosely if at all to behavioral data with the result that officials' opinions not only about their own power positions but about such matters as citizen participation or discrimination may simply be self-serving.

Advocacy Research and Policy Action

Based on this review of the literature and my understanding of federal decision-making processes, it might well be argued that the research most likely to have an impact upon policy makers, particularly if political attention and political controversy are joined together at a moment in time, is research with advocacy behind it. That research may be of two kinds: (1) formula research based on the analysis of complex statistical data; and (2) behavioral research closely tied to ethical values associated with assumptions about the desirability of nondiscrimination and citizen participation in local government.

Having employed something of a straw man up to now in the form of the notion of advocacy research, it may be useful to step back and question the dichotomy between advocacy research and what I have variously called "disinterested," "dispassionate," or "rigorous" research. The argument can well be made that every piece of research serves some interest beyond the research itself whether that interest is the promotion of the career of the researcher, the greater glory of the institution with which he or she is associated, or the pursuit of ideological or program-specific goals. A greater question might then become whether the advocacy is so central to the research that it either intentionally or unintentionally distorts the presentation or interpretation of data. Even such a formulation may assume too much, for at least from the perspective of certain schools of epistemology it is arguable whether there is such a thing as social and political "reality" or whether all research is necessarily the reporting of shadows on the cave walls. At a certain level of abstraction, perhaps it is just as well that most pieces of social research are sufficiently defective to make it possible for the political process to be selective in its use of research advice.

What may be of more immediate concern is the need to maintain a fairly open market in political research and political advice. One of the defects of the Johnson administration, as one recent study has suggested, was its passion for advice given in secret—advice that may or may not have been grounded in well-considered social research or an adequate understanding of the political process on the part of policy advisers.[5] In contrast, the many pieces of GRS research have been uneven in quality but at least they have operated in the open and made their findings and recommendations generally accessible.

One of the dangers that may arise in terms of the origins and sponsorship of policy research is that it will become too inbred. The issue is not simply one of an "old boy (or girl) network," although that may be of some concern where critical funding for social research goes to persons closely tied to what perhaps unfairly may be called the "federal bureaucracy–research institute complex." (Brookings and Rand are, of course, institutions that come immediately to mind in this connection; even more interesting, in some respects are the research wings of such bodies as the Advisory Commission on Intergovernmental Relations and the General Accounting Office.) No doubt, reciprocity exists in large part because the funding organization is aware that the researcher is capable of speaking both the social science and the political languages understood by actors in the policy process.

However, the problem in such a situation, as we should have learned from past experience, is that such researchers may too closely cut the cloth of their data collection processes and their recommendations to emphasize those proposals they perceive as being most acceptable to salient political actors. Fortunately, GRS has been a policy with enough ideological "play" to allow for a diversity of policy perspectives and alternative recommendations, some based on available data, others premised purely on individual understandings of how the intergovernmental system has operated or should operate in the United States. In areas such as foreign policy, one can think of numerous instances where policy analysts (including academics) assuming advocacy positions have played roles with consequences that have not served the public good.

In part, such policy errors have owed something to the narrowness of both the advisor base and the limitations of the research possible. All that one can do in such instances is hope that those who conduct policy research in areas of public concern assume a posture toward that research which allows findings to be analyzed separately from arguments in favor of the recommendations made. It also requires making participation in research an activity spread as widely as possible. Indeed, in a case like GRS it is fortunate that great interest in the subject generated a diversity of funding sources and made possible research that derived from often conflicting perspectives. Such a procedure is of course wasteful of intellectual resources, but perhaps that is a price that needs to be paid if research like the political process is to be opened to democratic participation. "Everyman" need not be a policy scientist but certainly the circle of those who participate in the research process should be maximized rather than being circumscribed to a few favored institutional outlets.

If this chapter does not constitute whole-hearted support of advocacy research as it presently operates, it is only because examples come to mind of such research that has cut itself off from use as serious policy analysis by the adoption of unsophisticated assumptions or the use of dubious methodologies.[t] What is necessary, albeit very difficult to achieve, is a form of research in which advocacy is integrated with methodologically sound efforts to identify and examine data sources. Enough "objectivity" is required to allow even a critic of any recommendations sufficient opportunity to distinguish sound mechanisms of policy research from what that critic may view as the bad policy advice given.

Notes

1. See, in particular, David Braybrooke and Charles E. Lindblom, *A Strategy of Decision* (New York: Free Press, 1963); Albert O. Hirschman, "The Principle of the Hiding Hand," *The Public Interest, #6* (Winter 1967), 10–23; Charles E. Lindblom, "The Science of Muddling Through," *Public Administration Review,* 19 (Spring 1959), 79–88; and Martin Meyerson and Edward C. Banfield, *Politics, Planning and the Public Interest* (Glencoe, Ill.: Free Press, 1955).

2. Daniel P. Moynihan, *Maximum Feasible Misunderstanding* (New York: Free Press, 1969), p. 177.

3. Ibid., p. 193.

4. Michael D. Reagan, *The New Federalism* (New York: Oxford University Press, 1972), and Lawrence Susskind, "Revenue Sharing and the Lessons of the New Federalism," *Urban Law Annual,* 8 (1974), pp. 33–71.

5. Bernard J. Frieden and Marshall Kaplan, *The Politics of Neglect* (Cambridge, Mass. and London, Eng.: MIT Press, 1975), p. 50.

---

[t] This formulation may give too much credit to "pure" policy research some of which may be questioned as readily for its sterility—a sterility resulting from the availability of quantifiable (albeit meaningless data sources); the desire to employ certain methodologies (sometimes apparently for their own sakes); or the frequent tendency to pursue "researchable" questions even when neither the questions nor the answers to those questions are intellectually interesting or particularly policy relevant.

9

General Revenue Sharing, Policy Analysis, and Fiscal Federalism: A Cautionary Note

David A. Caputo and Richard L. Cole

Public Law 92–512 (The State and Local Fiscal Assistance Act of 1972), or general revenue sharing, has indeed been a controversial piece of legislation. Not only has it stirred considerable political debate and controversy, it has also been responsible for considerable intellectual debate and discussion. The interesting aspect of the debate and discussion concerning general revenue sharing, whether by political or intellectual discussants, is that the conclusions reached are never totally correct or incorrect. That is, regardless of the position taken or point made, the ensuing discussion never results in an unrefutable point or a definitive position impervious to further analysis. Like "silly putty," the essence and impact of general revenue sharing for the American political system are difficult to grasp and even more difficult to document and explain fully. This results in conflicting sets of recommendations concerning the program, and raises some extremely important questions for policy evaluation research in general.

This chapter attempts to do several things. In the first place, the pro and con arguments used to justify the original general revenue sharing legislation are reconsidered in light of present empirical evidence and an attempt is made to determine if particular arguments are still applicable and justifiable in light of the program's four-year history. Second, several important empirical and normative questions involving the research community's response to the program are discussed and the general utility of the research that has resulted from that response is evaluated. Finally, general revenue sharing is considered from the perspectives of fiscal federalism and contemporary intergovernmental relations. This has not been systematically done elsewhere and is needed to provide the proper setting for the important theoretical points raised by the program.[a]

---

[a] For an attempt to raise these issues, see David A. Caputo, "General Revenue Sharing and American Federalism: Towards the Year 2000," in David A. Caputo, ed., *General Revenue Sharing and Federalism*, (May 1975) *Annals of the American Academy of Political and Social Science*, pp. 130–42.

161

Bofore proceeding, one final point should be made clear. As the previous chapters have indicated, general revenue sharing is not a neutral program randomly rewarding various groups within society. It is a program involving real fiscal resources to be allocated by publicly elected decision makers. The determination of who gets what, when, and how as a result of general revenue sharing has a considerable influence on research attempts. If a particular group has not done well under general revenue sharing, it becomes easier for the researcher to understand and accept that group's negative viewpoint. Similar explanations of positive behavior are also applicable. Readers might well consider their own set of values before proceeding so that the material can be consciously evaluated and considered in light of their personal underlying values and beliefs. This should provide a more realistic assessment of the program's actual and intended result.

Legislative Arguments

Since there have been numerous excellent summaries of the legislative history and development of the program,[1] these are not resummarized here. Instead, the main arguments as to the effects of general revenue sharing can be summarized as follows:

Pro

1. New unrestricted federal funds were needed to assist the cities in meeting the financial crises they were experiencing in the late 1960s and early 1970s.
2. General revenue sharing would provide the funds needed for new and innovative programs at the local level that would result in the elimination of pressing problems the categorical-aid programs of the 1960s could not solve.
3. "No-strings" federal funds would encourage increased responsiveness by local officials and citizens alike with the result being increased and more meaningful participation at the local level. The tendency to look to Washington for both money and approval of specific plans and projects would be reduced and local decision makers would have increased autonomy over their own sets of decisions and the implementation of policies they adopted.
4. The funds would not require a large administrative staff either in Washington or at the recipient level and therefore more funds would be available to deal with the problem and for providing services.

Con

1. Federal funds without detailed federal regulations and federal approval of their use would result in massive misuse of the funds by local officials. The funds would be used in frivolous ways and with little regard to the need to meet national standards in the areas of sewerage, environmental protection, or social services.

2. Since there were no provisions for citizen participation, individual and citizen group preferences would be ignored by those in decision-making positions without any concern over possible loss of funds. This would lead to decreased reliance on local government as the average citizen became more alienated with governmental action.

3. General revenue sharing would only encourage the larger cities to ignore the impending fiscal crisis. At some point the cities will have to make a series of tough choices regarding their services and financial commitments and general revenue sharing funds were viewed by some as increasing the possibility that cities could postpone those decisions for at least a short period.

4. The federal government, by making funds available to the local jurisdictions, would reduce the possibility of increased coordination and cooperation among them because they would have the financial resources they needed to remain independent. Carried to the extreme, general revenue sharing funds might even permit obsolete units of government to survive.

It should be obvious that any discussion of these pro and con arguments cannot ignore other aspects of federal domestic policy and events that directly affected the impact of general revenue sharing, but that were not caused by general revenue sharing. Several of the most important should be mentioned.

Certainly the entire web of mistrust and lack of action regarding a unified domestic policy from 1969 through 1974 had an impct on the recipient governments participating in general revenue sharing. The failure of the Nixon-Ford administrations to convince Congress that the proposed funding levels for a wide variety of domestic programs were adequate and the ensuing veto and veto override debates clearly indicate the conflict that existed concerning the essential aspects of domestic programs and policies. In spite of this "politics as usual" by Republican presidents and Democratic congresses, it was not the dominant influence on local governments in the United States during this time.

The dual economic problems of recession *and* inflation of the early 1970s created serious problems for the nation's local governments. Since the property tax is the primary source of revenue for local governments, the inflation of the 1970s made it difficult for these governments to continue to raise the revenues needed to meet not only increasing labor costs, but equipment and supply increases. While experiencing the results of inflation, the recession increased many of the demands made on these governments for services as the number of unemployed workers grew steadily. The result was, for many localities, a serious disruption of governmental services and benefits as demands increased while revenues declined. Thus, the double-barrel effect of recession and inflation contributed significantly to the environment for the upcoming debate concerning the renewal of general revenue sharing.

Table 9–1 summarizes the major pro and con arguments as indicated in the preceding discussion and summarizes the research reported by four major research efforts, the Brookings Institution monitoring project,[2] the Caputo–Cole study,[3] the Survey Research Center study,[b] and the general summary of the National Science Foundation's studies.[4] A close examination of table 9–1 reveals a variety of interesting and suggestive points concerning the actual impact of general revenue sharing.

As indicated in the table, the research results, in spite of different methodologies and approaches, are quite consistent. The only substantive disagreement comes on the contention that general revenue sharing would increase citizen participation. A closer examination of the Caputo–Cole conclusions[5] and the Goldenberg et al. conclusions[6] summarized in this book appear to reconcile these differences to a substantial degree. Based on these and other findings, it is safe to conclude

Table 9–1
Empirical Results of General Revenue Sharing

General Revenue Sharing Funds Would:	Brookings	Caputo–Cole	Survey Research Center	National Science Foundation
Pro				
Avert fiscal crisis	NA	+	+	+
Provide new programs	−	−	−	−
Increase citizen participation	−	+	−	−
Decrease administrative costs	NA	+	NA	NA
Con				
Result in misuse of funds	NA	−	−	−
Decrease city's responsibility	−	−	−	−
Decrease centralization tendencies	NA	NA	+	NA

Note: + indicates research results support this conclusion.
       − indicates research results do not support this conclusion.
       NA indicates research did not consider this question.

---

[b] These conclusions are based on the Edie N. Goldenberg, James W. Fossett, and Thomas J. Anton contributions to this book only.

that the bulk of the findings support a consistent set of results that provide support for a variety of both pro and con positions. Thus, one is left with the overall conclusion that the results of general revenue sharing have fully satisfied neither its advocates or critics and that future debate will be limited by these research findings.

Empirical and Normative Questions

Certainly one of the more interesting and unexpected results of general revenue sharing has been the large degree of research and academic attention the program has received. It is true that the program did affect the 50 states and the more than 37,000 units of local government that received funds under its provisions, but it could be argued that the voracity of the research community in pursuing general revenue sharing as a research topic has exceeded the impact the program may have had on the local governmental units. There are probably several reasons for this.

First, general revenue sharing was important not only as a specific program within the overall New Federalism framework, but also as a symbolic program indicating the direction of the Nixon–Ford administrations in domestic policy. The emphasis on decentralization to local decision makers with its tendency to increase the power of the local officials attracted academic attention and interest as it represented a perceived break with the centralizing tendencies of the older categorical-aid approach. The practical result was a tremendous amount of interest by academics in the new program.

One of the best examples of a careful, but speculative analysis of the probable impact of general revenue sharing conducted *prior* to the program's implementation was Michael Reagan's, *The New Federalism.*[7] Comparing the Nixon proposals with various aspects of the categorical-aid program, Reagan concluded that the changes were indeed important for American politics and that a basic philosophical belief—use of the categorical grant to achieve some form of national standard—would be hampered by the proposed changes.[8] Since Reagan's analysis was based on his assumptions of what would happen, it was logical that his writings served as testable hypotheses and research frameworks by others interested in exploring general revenue sharing. The important point is that general revenue sharing was the first of the New Federalism programs to receive congressional approval and thus became the empirical test for the normative claims often voiced by proponents and opponents of the New Federalism approach.

A second reason for the surge in revenue sharing interest was the ease of research access since all the local governments in the United States participated in the program. Often the laboratory was the researcher's own immediate surroundings. The researcher did not even need a state capital or the large city in order to undertake the research, instead, he had the test units required for a thorough investigation right before him. Undoubtedly this ease of access and wide applicablility contributed to the considerable amount of interest in the revenue sharing program.

Third, while general revenue sharing was important in and of itself, the process by which revenue sharing decisions were reached often shed considerable light on other important areas of local politics. For instance, the nature of the budgeting process could be investigated by an intensive focus on revenue sharing decisions. Or the impact of citizen participation in the decision-making process could be explored by concentrating on citizen participation during the general revenue sharing decision-making process. In addition, governmental response to new sources of funds and to governmental innovation could be investigated via general revenue sharing research. This last research approach has not been as widely pursued as it might have been and future research might be well advised to concentrate in this area. The point, however, is clear: general revenue sharing was not only a significant research topic itself, it also offered insights into other areas that have long had considerable appeal to researchers.

Finally, general revenue sharing received considerable research support from both governmental and private sources and this obviously heightened interest. As Trudi Lucas points out in chapter 6, the National Science Foundation devoted considerable time and attention to the program as well as a sizable amount of research funds. In addition, the Brookings Institution received considerable Ford Foundation support and a variety of public interest groups devoted considerable research effort and funds to the analysis and evaluation of the program.[c] The net result of this support was a wide variety of research by highly divergent groups of researchers. If ever did a "1,000 flowers bloom" in academic research, general revenue sharing was an excellent example of this phenomenon.

With this proliferation of research interests and methodologies, a variety of normative and empirical problems began to be widely discussed and debated. It is not our intent to summarize all of these problems (many have been pointed out in earlier chapters, especially chapter 8), but several do require consideration. Included among them is the question of fungibility, the problems of comparability, the absence of detailed case studies, and the lack of a sizable amount of longitudinal data. These points are raised not to be critical of current research in the area, but to point out the difficulties associated with undertaking this type of policy analysis and

---

[c] Probably best known among these was the League of Women Voter's study of community decision making under general revenue sharing.

that, in spite of the numerous and well-planned research efforts, sizable research gaps still exist.

Certainly the fungibility problem is familiar to most readers by now. Simply stated, it means that the researcher must be cautious in measuring how general revenue sharing funds were used because the reported usage (regardless of the respondent's intention) may not be correct. This can be due to a variety of factors, but most important is the fact that general revenue sharing can be used to replace other local funds that are then used elsewhere or simply not raised at all. Thus, the net impact of the funds would be missed by isolating only the initial allocations.

Various means have been devised to deal with the fungibility question—everything from asking observers to offer their best estimate as to the net effect of the funds[9] to sophisticated economic models that extrapolate prior budgetary decisions into the future with and without general revenue sharing funds.[d] The difficulty is that it is impossible (due to cost and time limitations) to consider the fungibility question in all recipient jurisdictions and the research to date that attempts to resolve this question often have had only very limited applicability.

The point here, however, is not that the fungibility question is inappropriate, but that it is not a new or unique question applicable only to general revenue sharing. Certainly the older categorical-aid programs created situations where recipient units of government could allocate local revenues "saved" by the availability of federal funds differently than they would have without the availability of the federal funds. *It is possible that the inordinate concern over the fungibility question has distracted attention from another basic question: who is in fact benefitting from the services provided by the receipt of general revenue sharing funds.* Are the funds being used to resolve local difficulties and improve services for the majority of residents or are they being used only to improve the conditions of a few? Obviously the question of fungibility enters in this discussion, but it is clearly a means to the end of understanding who benefits from general revenue sharing. The point here is that by concentrating so closely on the difficult task of "tracing" the funds, researchers may be ignoring other important questions that have greater policy relevance and applicability.

A similar problem is created by the absence of comparable data. This is bound to happen in a "laissez faire" research market and is not without advantages of its own, but the tremendous diversity of revenue sharing research has made it very difficult to compare various studies and to draw broad conclusions. This has meant that research findings are not as broadly applicable as one would hope and often are subject to considerable limitations and differing interpretations. This is due to two

---

[d] For an example of this approach, see Catherine Lovell et al., "The Effects of General Revenue Sharing on Ninety-Seven Cities in Southern California," NSF-RANN, volume 2.

reasons—the different jurisdictions involved and the differing methods of data gathering.

No two studies have actually used the exact same set of jurisdictions. For example, the Brookings study uses recipient jurisdiction of all types, the Caputo–Cole study, cities over 50,000; the Michigan study, cities over 25,000; the Wright study, state governments.[10] The problem is not that there are not a considerable number of interesting and important aggregate studies available, but that they do not involve the use of the same jurisdictions and thus it is difficult to compare the studies because their findings may in fact be due to different empirical reality and not just to the uniqueness of the study.

In similar fashion, the use of widely varying methodologies from phone surveys to in-depth personal observations also lead to problems of comparability. Thus, some criticism exists in the literature (see chapter 3) that casts doubt on a particular methodology or approach without considering the broader implications of that criticism for social science research in general. At some point someone may want to offer a cost–benefit analysis on the research done to date and consider whether the money invested in the various research projects has produced standardized benefits or whether there are wide discrepancies between the policy issues resolved in the research and the relevant cost involved.

A third (and for social scientists, an unusual) shortcoming of the research is the absence of many well-documented case studies. Considerable evidence exists as to the impact of general revenue sharing on various types and sizes of recipient jurisdictions, but little research has been done involving process oriented case studies. While we are not advocating case studies alone, the general revenue sharing renewal debate would profit from an increased understanding of the specific policy influences the funds have had in selected jurisdictions. What we presently have is an abundance of aggregated data that does not permit the researcher to investigate the dynamics of specific decision-making events and processes. Hopefully subsequent volumes of the Brookings study will help to fill this void as the field observers pull together their experiences.[11]

Finally, in spite of the considerable research effort concerning general revenue sharing, there is an absence of good longitudinal data. Certainly the Planned and Actual Use Reports can be used, but the major funding sources, including the National Science Foundation, have failed to support longitudinal research. The Brookings study and the Caputo–Cole city research are both longitudinal, but both have limitations due to the nature of the jurisdictions under investigation. In the future, researchers and funding agencies may want to consider a longer period when developing an empirical data base. Certainly one of the main criticisms of the NSF project is that it was too concerned with a single point in time and that greater attention should have been placed on the support of longitudinal studies permitting the investigation of the sustained impact of general revenue sharing.

In spite of these reservations and criticisms, the end result of the research effort to date is two-fold. On the one hand, those decision makers responsible for making the renewal decision can find substantial empirical evidence for just about any position they wish to take. The research results are so varied (sometimes even individual studies offer such a variety of viewpoints) that decision makers should easily be able to find evidence to support their points of view, regardless of what that view is. On the other hand, this should not concern researchers as they should be politically astute enough to realize that decision makers often seek and cite evidence to support and justify their political point of view and not to help them arrive at their position. Ultimately the willingness of decision makers to consider and understand research results defines the limits of policy analysis and research efforts for both the general revenue sharing program and public policy analysis in general. This does not mean that the researcher should not conduct his work in the most responsible and intellectually defensible way, but only that the limitations on the use of the results should be fully understood and considered by all interested parties. Thus, general revenue sharing and the research it has prompted must be understood in this context. As important as these questions may be, the real measure of general revenue sharing's impact may be in the area of its influence on American federalism. We conclude our chapter and this book with a consideration of this point.

Implications for Federalism

Perhaps the most important and often overlooked aspect of the entire general revenue sharing program has been its impact on intergovernmental relations in the United States and its influence in determining the nature of federalism in this country. If the research to date has a major theoretical omission, it would have to be its failure to assess realistically and completely this dimension of general revenue sharing. The reasons for this are many and varied, but to some extent it is due to the concern of many policy analysts that their work must be "value free" to the point that normative conclusions are not to be considered or investigated. We believe this is a major shortcoming and indeed could actually limit the utility and applicability of policy analysis research not only in general revenue sharing, but in general. In the next few pages we use our acquired knowledge from our own research experience as well as thoughts offered by the other researchers in the field to offer a series of observations about the implications of general revenue sharing for federalism in this country. Our expectation and hope is to encourage more sustained discussion about the broader theoretical and normative questions raised by general revenue sharing.[e]

In the first place, too much of the general revenue sharing research has tended to treat the program as if it existed in a vacuum and as if it were unaffected by other programmatic and societal shifts. Given the complexity of present economic conditions and municipal finances, it is difficult, time consuming, and perhaps even impossible to say with certainty the specific impact general revenue sharing has had on municipalities. Yet, a great deal of the research reaches such conclusions and either ignores the other diverse elements affecting local governments or underestimates their impact.

Numerous examples of this can be found in nearly all research efforts, but the most common error is to ignore the impact of general revenue sharing as it relates to the other decentralizing programs comprising the "New Federalism" of the Nixon–Ford administrations. Certainly the Community Development Legislation of 1974, the Comprehensive Employment Training Act, and the attempt to promote regionalism by the executive departments are all specific policy options that have had considerable impact on American institutions and public policy. Yet, little has been done in terms of trying to assess the role all of them together have played in affecting the quality of life in this country. Until general revenue sharing is put into this broader perspective, the utility of much of the present research will be limited.

This caveat is best illustrated by considering the present renewal debate on general revenue sharing. Even if one accepts the notion that the National Science Foundation supported research and other studies of general revenue sharing provide numerous examples of the possible effects of certain legislative choices, few of the research attempts will be of any assistance to the decision makers interested in considering their decision within the context of domestic policy parameters. Thus, these decision makers will be freed to reach conclusions based on specific analysis of general revenue sharing with the likelihood that their decisions will be more incremental than if they had been based on analysis stressing the contextual setting of the program and the overall impact of the New Federalism policy.

The danger of this is quite clear: by pursuing only limited policy analysis of a specific program, the researcher may be in the position to

---

[e] For examples, see Caputo, *General Revenue Sharing and Federalism;* and David O. Porter and Eugene A. Olsen, "Some Critical Issues in Government Centralization and Decentralization," *Public Administration Review,* 36 (January–February 1976), pp. 72–84.

offer important and useful suggestions regarding a specific policy option, but may be at a loss to offer a comprehensive plan to better the overall quality of life for citizens or to offer a series of coordinated policy choices for decision makers. If this obligation is disregarded or left to the political decision maker, the academic researcher has ignored a basic intellectual responsibility to understand and to analyze the broader implications of a particular policy or program. Let us hope that future policy analysts will be more sensitive to this particular need as they structure their research not only in the area of general revenue sharing, but in other areas as well.

Along with this absence of contextual analysis goes a preoccupation with official decision making. The National Science Foundation, except for a single limited phone survey, did not sponsor meaningful research into the impact of general revenue sharing on different recipient publics. This problem has two major dimensions and both deserve considerations.

In the first place, whether conscious or not, general revenue sharing was accompanied by a reduction in categorical-aid programs, which had its greatest impact on moderate- and low-income citizens. This in itself should have justified considerably more research into the actual recipients of services provided by general revenue sharing funds and by other sources of federal funding. In many respects, answers as to whether the funds were used for new or existing programs, whether the funds increased or decreased local taxes, whether most of the funds were spent for public safety or welfare needs, are less important than answers to the question of who actually was the final recipient of services funded by general revenue sharing money. Unfortunately, this research is time consuming and expensive and the research sponsors did not support proposals dealing with attempts to measure service deliveries. When it comes to final decisions on whether a program should or should not be continued decision makers may want answers to the very basic question of which groups have in fact received better services as a result of general revenue sharing. At present this information is lacking.

Second, the research has been too concerned with official response to general revenue sharing. This is understandable given the legislation's lack of specific citizen participation requirements, but except in isolated examples research is lacking that investigates the specifics of successful citizen involvement and even more important whether there are common elements as to why citizens did and did not try to exert influence over general revenue sharing decision making. Detailed elite surveys do not answer these questions and may even distort possible explanations of why there was not more citizen participation.

This emphasis on official response can be justified, but does seem to reflect a bias social scientists are often accused of reflecting. This is the emphasis on status quo and overt decisions at the expense of alternative research topics. This is not meant to criticize the researchers who have taken this approach, but only to point out the lack of a major effort in these areas that require careful investigation if general revenue sharing research is to be complete. This would be another major research emphasis for those pursuing general revenue sharing research in the future.

Closely related to these two points is another major criticism of a great deal of the research. In many cases, as has been pointed out, the specifics of the decision-making process have been ignored and we are left only with the results, which are not overly indicative of the conflict and turmoil that may have characterized the process. At the same time, reform advocates may be making an even more important mistake. By stressing process, in the form of required citizen participation hearings or other rules requiring specific "earmarking" of funds, they assume that procedural changes will lead to substantive changes also.

Thus, if one is displeased that such a large amount of the funds apparently are used for public safety and highway construction and maintenance, the assumption is that changing the allocation process will result in different allocation decisions. The problem is the assumption that process alone leads to substantive change. By concentrating on these procedural changes, reform advocates may be overlooking the absolute necessity for meaningful political organization and political development at the local level if local decision makers are to be influenced to reach different allocation decisions. The point should be quite clear and easily understood: procedural changes in and of themselves may not result in substantive changes and could result in reduced attempts to influence decisions because of the assumption that the procedural changes will automatically guarantee or improve the desired distribution of the funds. Thus, procedural changes alone, without the continuation of local political organization, could have a detrimental and opposite effect on those groups seen benefiting from a more open and accessible participatory process. Researchers should be more careful in pointing out the difficulty of this emphasis and should place their policy recommendations in a broader theoretical framework.

Finally, the ultimate test of general revenue sharing will be whether it does in fact influence the future course of American federalism. Obviously decentralization has been stressed in recent years, but there is considerable difference between decentralization to local authorities and decentralization to local citizens. The difference involves more than just practical questions of representation; it also includes major questions pertaining to basic rights and democratic values. While it seldom is discussed, the supporters of the Nixon proposal for general revenue sharing were not committed to returning the power to local citizens, but iather in returning the power to local decision makers supposedly representative of the people.

The problem here is major. If, as the community power research indicates, local governments are characterized by low citizen interest and often ruled by an economic or social minority,[f] the question then becomes one of whether increasing the resources at the disposal of local officials will really result in a different set of decisions. This broader question requires full consideration by the advocates of general revenue sharing as well as the researchers involved in policy analysis. The rhetoric of the program must be stripped and its reality investigated.

In closing this book, we encourage the reader to reconsider the various research attempts in light of these broader questions. If this is done, it should become clearer that policy analysis can in fact be a useful and important empirical approach for political scientists and that it may have significant importance for decision makers. However, its use as well as its users must also keep in mind a variety of critical, but often overlooked questions.

Notes

1. See David A. Caputo and Richard L. Cole, *Urban Politics and Decentralization: The Case of General Revenue Sharing* (Lexington, Mass.: Lexington Books, D.C. Heath and Co., 1974), pp. 17–66; Richard P. Nathan, Allen D. Manvel, and Susannah E. Calkins, *Monitoring Revenue Sharing* (Washington, D.C.: The Brookings Institution, 1974), pp. 13–36, 344–73; Paul R. Dommel, *The Politics of Revenue Sharing,* (Bloomington, Indiana: Indiana University Press, 1974); and Will S. Myers, "A Legislative History of Revenue Sharing," in David A. Caputo, ed., *General Revenue Sharing and Federalism,* (May 1975), *Annals of the American Academy of Political and Social Sciences,* pp. 1–11.

2. See Nathan, Manvel, and Calkins, *Monitoring Revenue Sharing,* pp. 37, 316.

3. Caputo and Cole, *Urban Politics,* pp. 67–160.

4. See National Science Foundation, *General Revenue Sharing Research Utilization Project,* volume 4, (Washington, D.C.: U.S. Government Printing Office, 1975), pp. v–x.

5. Caputo and Cole, *Urban Politics,* pp. 98–103.

6. Goldenberg, et. al., pp. 85–107.

---

[f] See, for instance, Robert A. Dahl, *Who Governs?* (New Haven: Yale University Press, 1961), pp. 163–65; and Floyd Hunter, *Community Power Structure* (New York: Anchor Books, 1963), pp. 61–112.

7. Michael D. Reagan, *The New Federalism* (New York: Oxford University Press, 1972).

8. Ibid., pp. 54–141.

9. See Nathan, Manvel, and Calkins, *Monitoring Revenue Sharing,* pp. 317–25.

10. Deil S. Wright and David Kovenack, "Assessing the Impact of General Revenue Sharing in the Fifty States: An Analysis Based on Participants' Perspectives," NSF-RANN, volume 2.

11. See Nathan, Manvel, and Calkins, *Monitoring Revenue Sharing,* pp. 279–308, for a preliminary discussion of these points.

Index

Index

About the Contributors

Thomas J. Anton is professor of political science and research scientist in the Institute of Public Policy Studies at The University of Michigan. A long-time student of budgeting, public policy-making, and comparative urban politics, he had major responsibilities in the two NSF-sponsored studies of General Revenue Sharing carried out on the Michigan campus. His latest book is *Governing Greater Stockholm: A Study of Policy Development and System Change* (Berkeley: University of California Press, 1975).

David Cozad is a candidate for the M.S. (Planning) degree from the Department of Urban and Regional Planning, Florida State University, and has held the position of Associate Director of the Institute for Social Policy Studies, Tallahassee, Florida since 1975. His major interests are in the social impact analysis of state tax and development policies. Mr. Cozad is an ordained Presbyterian minister and has also been working closely with church officials on the role of the church in working towards solutions for urban social problems.

Paul R. Dommel is associate professor of political science at Holy Cross College. His principal interest is public policy in general and urban policy in particular. He is the author of *The Politics of Revenue Sharing* and has published articles in *The New Republic* and the *Policy Studies Journal.* Professor Dommel is serving as a consultant to The Brookings Institution, researching the formula allocation system of the community development block grant program.

Kent Eklund received the B.A. from Augustana College, Rock Island, Illinois, in 1968 and the Ph.D. from the University of Pennsylvania in 1973. His dissertation topic was *The Politics of Suburban Land Use Controls.* He is assistant professor of political science at St. Olaf College, Northfield, Minnesota. The research reported in the article appearing in this volume, as well as several forthcoming articles, was supported by a National Science Foundation Grant jointly administered with Professor Williams. In addition to continuing personal research in varieties of questions related to suburban politics, Professor Eklund has served as a consultant for the Metropolitan Council of the Twin Cities and is a member of the Rice County Planning and Zoning Board.

James W. Fossett is a graduate student in political science at The University of Michigan, specializing in intergovernmental relations and urban politics. He has been employed by the Georgia State Merit System and has published research on the impact of general revenue sharing on local decision making.

Edie N. Goldenberg is an assistant professor of political science and associate in the Institute of Public Policy Studies and the Institute for Social Research at The University of Michigan. She was a contributor to *The Economic and Political Impact of General Revenue Sharing,* edited by F. Thomas Juster (Washington, D.C.: Government Printing Office, forthcoming). Her other recent work includes *Making the Papers: The Access of Resource-Poor Groups to the Metropolitan Press* (Lexington, Massachusetts: Lexington Books, 1975).

Catherine Lovell is an assistant professor in the Graduate School of Administration, University of California, Riverside. Her research interests are centered on local government finance. She was the Principle Investigator on a National Science Foundation funded study of the effects of General Revenue Sharing on 97 Southern California cities. Professor Lovell is serving as a Field Associate for the Brookings Institution on their study of the Community Development Block Grant program.

Trudi Lucas is a program manager in RANN, the Research Applications Directorate of the National Science Foundation. Her degree is in Political Science from the University of North Carolina. Before coming to the Foundation she was an assistant professor at SUNY-Buffalo and a guest scholar at the Brookings Institution. Professor Lucas is on detail from RANN to U.C. Berkeley where she is working on a manuscript which develops ideas that are sketched out in this volume. Specifically, she is exploring the joint implications for policy research of pluralistic democratic models and the philosophy of science. The manuscript will include examples of the confusion of values and methods in basic and applied research and descriptions of recent attempts in applied research management to make assumptions explicit. She will return to RANN in November, 1976.

Donald B. Rosenthal is a professor of political science at the State University of New York at Buffalo. His research and teaching interests include local politics and intergovernmental relations in both the United States and South Asia. Among his publications are *The Politics of Community Conflict, The Limited Elite* and *The City in Indian Politics.* A study of rural politics in the Indian state of Maharashtra will soon be published. Along with a number of articles in professional journals, he has recently published *Local Power and Comparative Politics* (with Mark

Kesselman). Professor Rosenthal was associated with the research project on general revenue sharing sponsored by the RANN Division of the National Science Foundation. He is presently conducting research on intergovernmental decision-making for the Buffalo metropolitan area.

Richard A. Smith is an assistant professor, Department of Urban and Regional Planning, Florida State University. Previously an instructor at Cornell University (1970–1972) where he also received the Ph.D. (Urban Planning–1973) and M.R.P. (1965) degrees. Professional positions include the Planning Department, Greater London Council, London, England (1965–1967). Recent publications are as follows: "Measuring Neighborhood Cohesion: A Review and Some Suggestions," *Human Ecology,* 3 (July 1975); "Social Scientists in the Policy Process," *Journal of Applied Behavioral Sciences* 12 (Winter 1976); "Community Power and Decision Making: Replication and Extension of Hawley," *American Sociological Review* 14 (August 1976). Professor Smith's general research interests include community structure and policy processes, the sociology of neighborhoods and housing segregation.

Alvin D. Sokolow is associate professor of political science at the University of California, Davis, and associate director of the Institute of Governmental Affairs. He received the Ph.D. in political science (1964) from the University of Illinois. His articles on state legislative politics and policy making have been published in *Western Political Quarterly, Harvard Journal on Legislation, National Civic Review, California Journal* and other journals. Professor Sokolow is coauthor of a book on California government and politics and author of a monograph on *Governmental Response to Urbanization.* He is writing two books, one on small community politics and policy making and the other on the impact of reapportionment on the California legislature.

Oliver P. Williams is professor of political science at the University of Pennsylvania, and a specialist in urban politics. He is the author of *Metropolitan Political Analysis,* and coauthor of *Suburban Differences & Metropolitan Policies* and *Four Cities.* He is engaged in a N.S.F. supported research project in collaboration with Kent Eklund on the changing structure of political units in the Philadelphia metropolitan area.

About the Editors

David A. Caputo is associate professor of political science, Purdue University where he teaches courses in urban politics and intergovernmental relations. He is the author of *Urban America: The Policy Alternatives* (W. H. Freeman, 1976), *American Politics and Public Policy: An Introduction* (J. B. Lippencott, 1974), and a coauthor of *Urban Politics and Decentralization: The Case of General Revenue Sharing* (Lexington Books, 1974) as well as editing symposiums dealing with general revenue sharing in the *Annals of the American Academy* and the *Public Administration Review.* Professor Caputo has contributed to the *Midwest Journal of Political Science, Publius, Policy Sciences, Urban Affairs Quarterly* and the *1974 Municipal Year Book.*

Richard L. Cole is assistant professor of political science at George Washington University where he teaches courses in urban politics, state politics, and political methodology. He is the author of *Citizen Participation and the Urban Policy Process* (Lexington Books, 1974) and a coauthor of *Urban Politics and Decentralization: The Case of General Revenue Sharing* (Lexington Books, 1974). He has contributed to the *Midwest Journal of Political Science, 1974 Municipal Year Book, Publius, Social Science Quarterly, Tax Review, Urban Affairs Quarterly,* and the *American Journal of Political Science.*